Living in the Power and Realm of The Holy Spirit

By
Brian Reddish

Living in the Power and Realm of The Holy Spirit

© **2021 by Brian Reddish**
ISBN 978-1-8384255-3-1
Published by Caracal Books-United Kingdom
https://www.facebook.com/CaracalBooks/

All rights reserved. No part of this publication may be reproduced, stored in a retrieval system, or transmitted in any form or by any means — for example, electronic, photocopy, recording — without the prior written permission of the publisher. The only exception is brief quotations in printed reviews.

The internet addresses, email addresses, and phone numbers in this book are accurate at the time of publication.

Cover photo: www.shutterstock.com

Green Light-Eliks   Bible-Richard Lowthian

Unless otherwise indicated, all Scripture taken from the New King James Version®. Copyright © 1982 by Thomas Nelson. Used by permission. All rights reserved.

INTRODUCTION

Living in the Power and Realm of The Holy Spirit

Coming to God by believing in His Son opens the door to the most amazing life possible! This book addresses The Holy Spirit's work in the daily life of the child of God and how He works in unison with the Word of God beginning at spiritual birth reaching full maturity. Right from the outset, The Holy Spirit is involved in bringing us to Christ through faith in God's Word.
DID YOU KNOW ?

The moment a person receives Jesus, a massive spiritual transformation takes place in Heaven and each one of us? Jesus calls it being BORN AGAIN! The Bible says we are transferred from the kingdom of darkness into the kingdom of light. That is into GOD'S KINGDOM!

> *"He has delivered us from the power of darkness and conveyed us into the kingdom of the Son"*
> **Colossians 1: 13**

Thereafter, Each child of God is commanded to,
> *"...grow in the grace and knowledge of our Lord and Saviour Jesus Christ."*
> **2 Peter 3:18**

and to,
> *"... desire the pure milk of the Word that you may grow thereby."*

1 Peter 2:2

And so, the journey begins. Throughout our entire life, The Holy Spirit is with us, teaching us, leading us, comforting us, empowering us and sanctifying us until we reach a state of maturity, fulfilling His calling and will for our lives.

Our personal relationship with God is the most important aspect of our life. When our life upon earth has ended, it will still go on forever, living eternally with God! Therefore, during our lifetime, our personal knowledge and acceptance of God's Word, as recorded in the Bible, together with our relationship with The Holy Spirit, is so vital!

It is The Holy Spirit who makes God real to us. It is He who teaches and leads us to know the Truth by testifying to Jesus Christ. Most importantly, The Holy Spirit opens our understanding of the Word of God and empowers us to be a witness to the lost!

So, we will need to ask the following questions.

- What does the Bible say and teach about the Holy Spirit?
- What does Jesus Himself teach and say about the Holy Spirit?
- What does it mean to Walk in The Spirit?

Why is it, one may ask, that the third Person of the Godhead can often be the least known and understood?

This book will hopefully change all of that!

Brian Reddish
March 2021

Living in the Power and Realm of The Holy Spirit

PART 1 *A New Life*
Chapter 1 - A Ruler called Nicodemus
Chapter 2 - Nicodemus, Signs and Wonders
Chapter 3 - You Must be Born Again!
Chapter 4 - Nicodemus said to Jesus
Chapter 5 - You Must be born again …born of water and The Spirit
Chapter 6 - What Does it Mean to Repent?
Chapter 7 - The Flesh
Chapter 8 - The Spirit

PART 2 *A New Purpose*
Chapter 9 - The Call of Abraham
Chapter 10 - Abraham's Challenge
Chapter 11 - Choices and Decisions
Chapter 12 - The Flesh and The Spirit
Chapter 13 - Abraham and Lot

PART 3 *Learning to Walk with God*
Chapter 14 - Denying Yourself
Chapter 15 - Being Alone with God
Chapter 16 - Jesus Christ is My Lord
Chapter 17 - The Fountain of Living Water
Chapter 18 - Desire the Pure Milk of the Word
Chapter 19 - The Bread of Life

PART 4   *The Holy Spirit*
Chapter 20 - A Prophecy
Chapter 21a – Living in the Power and Realm of The Holy Spirit
Chapter 21b - His Purpose
Chapter 22 - The Spirit Bestows His Gifts
Chapter 23 - Walking in The Spirit – 1
Chapter 24 - Walking in The Spirit – 2
Chapter 25 - Sanctification of The Spirit

PART 5 –   *God's Eternal Laws*
Chapter 26 - Thinking Differently - Kingdom Laws
Chapter 27 - God's Conditional Promises
Chapter 28 - Will A Man Rob God?

PART 6 -   *Seated with Christ*
Chapter 29 - There is Power in the Name of Jesus
Chapter 30 - Confessing the Name of Jesus
Chapter 31 - Our Position Seated with Christ in the Heavenly Places

PART 1

A New Life

DAY 1

A Ruler called Nicodemus

*There was a man of the Pharisees named Nicodemus, a ruler of the Jews. This man came to Jesus by night and said to Him, "Rabbi, we know that **You are a teacher come from God;** for no one can do these signs that You do unless God is with him."*

John3:1-2

We will learn a lot from these two verses from John's Gospel as we take the time to pause, look and contemplate! It was near the beginning of Jesus' ministry.

"Who was He?" some would ask.

"Is this not Joseph the carpenter's son?" said others.

It was later on in His ministry when Jesus came into the region of Caesarea Philippi with His disciples that He asked them a similar question,

"Who do men say that I, the Son of Man, am?"

> So, they said, "Some say John the Baptist, some Elijah, and others Jeremiah or one of the prophets."
> He said to them, **"But who do you say that I am?"**
> Simon, called Peter, answered and said, "You are the Christ, the Son of the living God."
> Jesus answered and said to him, "Blessed are you, Simon Bar-Jonah, for **flesh and blood has not revealed this to you, but My Father who is in Heaven."**
>
> **Matthew 16: 13b -17**

The answer Jesus gave to Peter is of profound importance as it relates, not to human understanding (flesh and blood) but Divine illumination from God Himself! (by The Holy Spirit.)

Immediately, we face the question, *"Can no one possibly understand who Jesus is except it is revealed to them by God Himself?"*

Nicodemus was a high-ranking ruler of the Jews and, as a Pharisee, would have been a member of the Sanhedrin. He was, you might say, a scholar of the Law, but he did not know who Jesus was. This demonstrates that acquiring a religious education with status and position and having an excellent human understanding of the Scriptures alone does not necessarily open our eyes to spiritual things! We can possess academic knowledge, but that's it. Nicodemus needed God to open his eyes just like God had opened those of Peter and, as we shall see, every person likewise is in precisely the same predicament! We all need God to open our eyes spiritually to see Jesus and recognise who He is!

The following Scripture passages should encourage most of us because of what is written.

> *"At that time Jesus answered and said, "I thank You, Father, Lord of heaven and earth, that **You have hidden these things from the wise and prudent and have revealed them to babes.** Even so, Father, for so it seemed good in Your sight."*
>
> **Matthew 11: 25-27**

And furthermore still,

> *"For you see your calling, brethren, that not many wise according to the flesh, not many mighty, not many noble, are called. But **God has chosen the foolish things of the world to put to shame the wise, and God has chosen the weak things of the world to put to shame the things which are mighty; and the base things of the world and the things which are despised God has chosen, and the things which are not, to bring to nothing the things that are, that no flesh should glory in His presence."***
>
> **1 Corinthians 1:26-29**

What was it that first captured the interest and curiosity of Nicodemus regarding the Person of Jesus? The Scripture at the beginning of today's reading tells us just what had drawn him to come and see Jesus in Person, howbeit, we observe that it was at night out of sight of all others. Was he afraid to talk to Jesus at any other time of the day? Was he afraid to be seen by others associating himself with Jesus, for it was common knowledge that the Pharisees resented Jesus and His teachings?

Nicodemus, being himself a teacher, immediately recognised two qualities in Jesus. He saw that He was a teacher and that He must have come from God! Combining these two attributes, he acknowledged, therefore, something extraordinary in Jesus, something that he could never attain.

> *"Rabbi, we know that You are a teacher come from God."*

On other occasions, people marvelled at the wisdom and knowledge of Jesus but with one added quality that distinguished Him from all others, namely, Jesus spoke with **authority.**

> *"And so, it was, when Jesus had ended these sayings, that the people were astonished at His teaching, for He taught them as **one having authority, and not as the scribes.**"*
> **Matthew 7: 28-29**

The Jews marvelled at the words of Jesus when He spoke in the Temple.

> *"Now about the middle of the feast Jesus went up into the temple and taught. And the Jews marvelled, saying,* **"How does this Man know letters, having never studied?"**
>
> **John 7: 14-15**

Jesus' manner of teaching amazed people, grasping their attention with amazement, conviction, persuasion and influence Moreover, Jesus spoke with authority, speaking as from God and not from mere man. This challenged Nicodemus! Jesus was different; He was, by far, different from him!

Who is Jesus to you?

> *Open the eyes of my heart, Lord*
> *Open the eyes of my heart*
> *I want to see You*
> *I want to see You*

Open the Eyes of My Heart lyrics © Capitol Christian Music Group

Meditation

Nicodemus helps bury Jesus in Joseph of Arimathea's Tomb

After this, Joseph of Arimathea, being a disciple of Jesus, but secretly, for fear of the Jews, asked Pilate that he might take away the body of Jesus; and Pilate gave him permission. So, he came and took the body of Jesus. ***And Nicodemus, who at first came to Jesus by night, also came, bringing a mixture of myrrh and aloes, about a hundred pounds.*** *Then* ***they*** *took the body of Jesus, and bound it in strips of linen with the spices, as the custom of the Jews is to bury.*
John 19: 38-40

DAY 2

Nicodemus, Signs and Wonders

There was a man of the Pharisees named Nicodemus, a ruler of the Jews. This man came to Jesus by night and said to Him, "Rabbi, we know that You are a teacher come from God; ***for no one can do these signs (miracles) that You do unless God is with him."***

John 3:1-2

The second thing that caught Nicodemus' attention was the signs (miracles) Jesus performed before the crowds. Clearly, Nicodemus' reasoning was this,

"…no one can do these signs (miracles) that You do unless God is with him."

It was true; everywhere Jesus went, there were miracles! On one occasion, John the Baptist's disciples enquired of Jesus whether He was the one to come or should they be looking for another.

> *"Jesus answered and said to them, (for that very **hour He had cured many of infirmities, afflictions, and evil spirits; and to many blind, He gave sight**,)* "*Go and tell John the things you have seen and heard: that **the blind see, the lame walk, the lepers are cleansed, the deaf hear, the dead are raised, the poor have The Gospel preached to them…*"
>
> **Luke 7:21-22**

After Jesus had been baptised by John earlier, He went in the Power of The Holy Spirit and, beginning at Galilee, started His ministry. News of Him spread quickly through all the surrounding regions. It was when He went into the Temple at Nazareth, however, that Jesus faced severe opposition. You see, Jesus had picked up the book of Isaiah and read out the following to them:

> *"The Spirit of The Lord God is upon Me, Because The Lord has anointed Me To preach good tidings to the poor; He has sent Me to heal the brokenhearted, to proclaim liberty to the captives, and the opening of the prison to those who are bound…"*
>
> **Isaiah 61:1**

Jesus declared that the above prophecy was fulfilled before their very eyes, but this was not what they wished to hear! Miracles, yes! Turning water into wine, yes! Creating bread and fish enough to feed five thousand, yes! - but not this! So, they murmured, saying, **"Is this not Joseph's son?"**

After Jesus reproved those in the Temple, they were *filled with wrath* and took Him outside and would have killed Him there and then by throwing Him over a hilltop, but Jesus walked away, and they did not touch Him!

On another occasion, Jesus appeared to react adversely when pressed for signs and wonders. Why was this, we might ask ourselves?

John's Gospel tells us,

> *"Jesus came again to Cana of Galilee where he had made water into wine and there was a certain nobleman whose son was sick at Capernaum and when he heard that Jesus had come out of Judea into Galilee, he went to him, and implored him to come down and heal his son, for he was at the point of death. Then Jesus said to him,* **Unless you people see signs and wonders, you will by no means believe...go your way,** *said Jesus, for your son lives.*
>
> **John 4:46-48**

The healing of this nobleman's son not only demonstrates Jesus' power to heal, but it highlights the principle that He did not regard signs and wonders as ends in themselves. Jesus expected more from them, seeing as it was, He in their midst! This was no less highlighted when Jesus rebuked certain cities local to Galilee for not receiving Him despite all the wonderful works He did there.

> *"And you, Capernaum, who are exalted to heaven, will be brought down to Hades; for if the mighty works which were done in you had been done in Sodom, it would have remained until this day. But I say to you that it shall be more tolerable for the land of Sodom in the day of judgment than for you."*
>
> **Matthew 11: 23-24**

The above passage is a stark warning to those who have received much from God but remain impenitent, complacent or unmoved to follow Him wholeheartedly! Again, the words of Jesus come to mind when He said,

> *"...For everyone to whom much is given, from him much will be required; and to whom much has been committed, of him they will ask the more*
>
> **Luke 12: 48b**

Jesus saw the grave reality! It was this; man would die one day without salvation through Him and be lost for all Eternity. The death sentence was upon all mankind, and Jesus, knowing full well His mission sought to call man to believe upon Him! He alone was the way, the only way! Physical healing of the body is a great blessing but a temporary remedy nevertheless. It cannot, in itself, provide for salvation from the guilt and punishment of sin. No, Jesus was aware that He was to be the sacrifice for sin. So His overriding desire and purpose were to do The Father's will, pointing people to believe in Him and not insist upon signs and wonders alone, which is a matter we should think about seriously when it comes to our priorities in life and expectations from God.

Furthermore, Jesus saw that in the future, not all signs and wonders would come from God, which He pointed out to them on another occasion when He said:

*"For false Christs and false prophets will arise and **show signs and wonders to deceive**, if possible, even the elect. But take heed, I have told you beforehand."*

Mark 13:22-23

Signs and wonders are spectacular and very persuasive, but in the wrong hands can easily divert people's attention from God, appeasing the flesh only. Jesus saw this, and whilst He desired to perform miracles to bless people, His priority was to focus upon saving souls! That's why Jesus desires us to believe in Him first and foremost. Signs and wonders are only to be used as a means of drawing people to believe in God.

We should be wise and careful. Yes! of course, God heals! God saves! God delivers! In fact, Jesus sent His disciples to heal the sick and perform many miracles and wonders in His name, and today, He can use you and me to do likewise through His Spirit's power working through us when we pray by faith in the Name of Jesus! Even so, let us always remember that the most important thing is the healing of the soul and the assurance of eternal life with Christ in Heaven!

We only know and experience life here and now and so cannot always easily appreciate the above! God, however, sees the bigger picture. He sees our lives from beginning to end. All sickness is a burden. God's Word tells us to pray for the sick and talks of spiritual gifts of healing.

Who knows, we may mature and be strengthened when we endure hardships? On '**That Day**', we shall look back and say, "It was worth it all to see Jesus!" Meanwhile, we are all called to live by faith and trust God in every circumstance, for He has said,

"I will never leave you or forsake you."
Hebrews 13:5

After Jesus had performed the miracle of feeding the five thousand, He perceived that they were about to come and take Him by force to make Him king, so He departed and went to pray in a mountain alone. Once again, we see a problem of diversion and distraction regarding the ministry of Jesus as a direct result of the miracle He had performed! Furthermore still, there is even more! Upon returning to that same region the following day, Jesus saw that many people were searching for Him, seeking Him, asking the question, *"Where is He?"*
Jesus answered them and said,

> *"Most assuredly, I say to you, you seek Me, not because you saw the signs, **but because you ate of the loaves and were filled.** Do not labour for the food which perishes, but for the food which endures to everlasting life, which the Son of Man will give you …"*
> **John 6: 26-27**

They just wanted the bread! People can be distracted entirely away from the prime mission of Jesus, but such is human nature. Miracles that meet our needs in this life are always most welcome, is that not so?

Finally, we praise God for his grace that does meet our needs when we are sick or have a situation that requires His miraculous hand. We are encouraged to pray and let our requests be made known to God. Remember this special promise,

> **"Jesus Christ is the same yesterday, today and forever.**

Hebrews 13:8

Thoughts and Meditation

"Believe Me (Jesus) that I am in The Father and The Father in Me, or else believe Me for the sake of the works themselves."

John 14:11

Jehovah Rapha – *"I am The Lord who heals you."*

Exodus 15:23b

Prayer

Thank You, Lord Jesus, for coming to this earth to live and die for me! You saw not only my temporal needs but those of Eternity too! I now understand this much more clearly than before. I desire Your priorities to be mine and seek You first above all things and not just for what I wish. Teach me Your ways and show me Your paths.

DAY 3

"You Must be Born Again!"

> *"Most assuredly, I (Jesus) say to you, (Nicodemus)* **unless one is born again, he** *cannot see the kingdom of God."*
>
> **John 3:4**

Jesus answered Nicodemus in a way that seemingly did not address his line of reasoning. Instead, Jesus spoke of Nicodemus' fundamental root need, and indeed, that of every human being for that matter. It was simply this,

> *"...unless one is born again, he cannot see the Kingdom of God!"*

This reply of Jesus has ramifications, consequences, and implications for everyone without respect of persons. Nicodemus was certainly no exception, and there was no compromise in the mind of Jesus regarding this earthly religious teacher of great prominence. Think of it for just a moment; Kings and Queens, Emperors, billionaires, Archbishops, Priests, Popes, "righteous living" and "upright people" … they all need to be born again; along with everyone else if they are to see the Kingdom of God! Does this surprise you? Perhaps not for the Bible says,

> *"... for all have sinned and fall short of the glory of God."*
>
> **Romans 3:23**

Nicodemus clearly had an intellectual problem with the reply he received, but Jesus left no room for uncertainty when He declared to him,

> **"Do not marvel that I said to you, you must be born again."**
>
> **John 3:7**

In other words,

> *"...do not be surprised that I am telling you this!"*

Note that this is a command from God when it says, *"You **must** be born again."* Why is this so necessary? Why is this so important?

It is imperative that we all consider this truth very carefully, especially regarding our self! Remember, it goes without saying that each and every Word of God that directly involves me personally is of paramount importance and cannot be brushed aside. In other words, our attitude ought to be:

Jesus said it, I believe it, and that settles it!

We will look at this command of Jesus in detail and see the many glorious truths that will unfold for every believer in Christ as a result of being born again, but for now, we will dwell on the actual statement itself.

Firstly, Jesus began by saying to Nicodemus the words – *"Most assuredly…"*

This can be correctly translated as *verily, verily* or *truly, truly.*[1]

(N.B. The Latin word for *truth* is *veritas* from which the word verily is derived)

In each case, there is a double emphasis which is a declaration of **unchanging, absolute truth**. It is a Divine truth that must be accepted. It is both absolute and foundational, so it cannot be altered or changed.

The Greek for the word *again* can be equally translated as *from above* [2] so that the verse could read,

> *" …unless one is born FROM ABOVE, he cannot see the kingdom of God."*

We will see that this refers to being born *of God* or The Holy Spirit. In other words, Jesus declares that to belong to the Kingdom of God, a person requires a change. This inner spiritual change comes about directly from God Himself working in the believer, and it is not the work of man, which is made very clear in the verses below,

> *"…as many as **received** Him, (Jesus) to them He gave the right to become children of God, to those who **believe** in His name: **who were born, not of blood, nor of the will of the flesh, nor of the will of man, but of God.**"*
>
> **John 1: 12-13**

[1] Strong's Cocordance

[2] Strong's Concordance

How does this come about? The Gospel (*Good News*) of Jesus Christ is very clear. It is only trusting in His shed blood upon the cross that saves a person. It entails believing that Jesus died for your sins and that you have **received** this free gift for yourself. There is a subtle difference worth highlighting by using an example to illustrate what is meant by both believing and receiving. We shall see that *believing and receiving* go hand in hand.

If I hold up a £10 note and ask you the question, *"Do you **believe** this is a £10 note?"*

You will say: *"Yes, it looks like one!"*

If I then ask you who it belongs to, you will say, *"It is Yours!"*

If I hold it out to give to you, you will unhesitatingly take it and respond, saying, *"Thank you!"*

Now I tell you that *the £10 note is yours!*

Clearly, the person had to **believe** it was real then reach out and **receive** the £10 note for themselves – a meeting of mind and heart! Therefore, an action was required apart from just believing, leading to acceptance! In other words, *I **believe** it is a £10 note, and I **receive** it for myself!*

It is vital we understand that believing in Jesus and receiving Him for ourselves go together. Believing in Jesus is not to be merely an intellectual acceptance of who He is. Even Nicodemus recognised that God must have sent Jesus, but he was far from receiving Jesus personally upon that occasion!

In this book, we shall see that God does not desire a distant relationship with us but, on the contrary, a close and personal relationship! How do you feel about that?

Prayer and Confession to God

Lord Jesus, I confess that up until now, I have mostly known about You in the form of knowledge – but nothing more! I now realise that there is much more for me! I feel like I need to come in closer. I desire to be "born again" as You have stated emphatically in Your Word that I must be!

Prayer to be Born again

Lord Jesus, I believe that You are the Son of God and that You died upon the cross paying the price for my sins so that I can now be forgiven through my repentance and acknowledgment of my sin.
I believe upon You as my God and Saviour, and I receive You for myself. Please come into my heart and life in a real way and teach me the way I should now live through Your Word.
Amen.

DAY 4

Nicodemus said to Jesus,

"How can a man be born when he is old? Can he enter a second time into his mother's womb and be born?

John 3:4

Nicodemus clearly didn't understand what Jesus meant as he replied with an answer of total bewilderment!

"How can a man be born when he is old? Can he enter a second time into his mother's womb and be born?"

Yet, Nicodemus was not a dimwit as one might at first suppose! Notice in his answer to Jesus how he speaks of, " ... *when he is old."*

The dilemma regarding entering into your mother's womb a second time and being born would be the same whether the person was young or old, would it not? This leads us to suppose that Nicodemus may have already been old at the time and that he was specifically thinking of himself and how he could change at his age and time of life to start over!

As already stated, Nicodemus was not naive! He was a teacher of the Law. Jesus later referred to Nicodemus as *the teacher of Israel,* and he must have been familiar with the odd metaphor now and again! Even so, sometimes there are none more unlearned than the learned, and both must desire wisdom from Christ only!

Does Nicodemus understand Jesus to mean that no one is good enough to enter the kingdom and that all must start afresh in some new way or other? Nicodemus thinks Jesus is going too far.

> *Are you really saying that people need to start over again in life somehow (it's a bit late for me!) and have a new beginning following some new prescribed way?*

Nicodemus, being old, would be daunted at the prospect of another lifetime of change, especially since Jesus was advocating that being born again was necessary to see the Kingdom of God.

Jesus faced such bewilderment and perplexity on other occasions whilst teaching the people about the Kingdom, and the following passage illustrates this well.

> *"It is easier for a camel to go through the eye of a needle than for a rich man to enter the kingdom of God."*
> *And they were greatly astonished, saying among themselves, "Who then can be saved?"*
> *But Jesus looked at them and said,* **"With men it impossible, but not with God; for with God all things are possible."**
> **Mark 10: 25-27**

Perhaps one of the most significant challenges Jesus encountered was with His disciples and followers, as is revealed in the passage below.

> "Most assuredly, I say to you, unless you eat the flesh of the Son of Man and drink His blood, you have no life in you. Whoever eats My flesh and drinks My blood has eternal life, and I will raise him up at the last day. For My flesh is food indeed, and My blood is drink indeed. He who eats My flesh and drinks My blood abides in Me, and I in him."
>
> **John 6: 53-56**

> "Therefore, many of His disciples, when they heard this, said, **this is a hard saying; who can understand it?"**
>
> **John 6: 60**

This passage is clearly figurative because Jesus is referring to Himself. Jesus is talking about an intimate relationship of man with Himself.

> "He who eats My flesh and drinks My blood **abides in Me, and I in him."**

Jesus spoke of the importance of abiding in Him elsewhere.

> "Abide in Me, (the vine) and I in you. As the branch cannot bear fruit of itself, unless it abides in the vine, neither can you, unless you abide in Me."
>
> **John 15:4**

Jesus is not, literally, a vine but, in comparing himself to such, declares that He is The Spiritual source of life and sustenance to each branch (or believer) that abides in Him.

> *"It is The Spirit who gives life; the flesh profits nothing. The words that I speak to you are spirit, and they are life."*
>
> **John 6:63**

Jesus highlights the vast gulf in man's reasoning and lack of understanding regarding the truth and knowledge of God without The Spirit's illumination. It is so far above man's human capacity to even begin to know The Spirit sphere and realm of life within which God lives and reigns supreme. Therefore, without apology, Jesus teaches of the greater inner need of man, to be *born again, not of the flesh, nor of the will of man but of God.* God requires this. Nothing else will suffice; it is a foundational truth. God desires for us to know Him and His Word at a spiritual and more intimate level, and man cannot of himself attain to this however he may try. This Jesus sums up, in the latter passage, teaching about Himself as the source of all spiritual life, knowledge, and understanding!

We can often erroneously think that the more we read the Bible and participate in church attendance, religious ordinances and the like, the more we will grow and understand the things of God.

Not necessarily so! If we are not born again and filled with The Spirit, how can we ever engage in the living reality of knowing God personally in our life? How can we ever appropriate God's Word without the help of the author, The Holy Spirit, who inspired it? God is a spirit, and we can only spiritually relate to Him. Hence Jesus insists, *you must be born again!*

It is foundational! It is essential if we are to see the Kingdom of God. However, knowing full well that man will soon be able to access through Him the very presence of God by The Spirit, Jesus pursues His quest and mission to press for higher things from man's faith by continually referring to the things of The Spirit – even to a lone woman of Samaria at a well!

> *"Jesus said to her, "Woman, believe Me, the hour is coming when you will neither on this mountain, nor in Jerusalem, worship The Father...But the hour is coming, and now is, when the **true worshipers will worship The Father in spirit and truth; for The Father is seeking such to worship Him. God is Spirit, and those who worship Him must worship in spirit and truth.**"*
> **John 4:21, 23-24**

Observe the earnest love and God's desire for man to enter His presence - *for The Father is seeking such to worship Him!* If a man is to be born again, it is that he may enter into fellowship with none other than God Himself! How much has religion become dry and stale, forgetting this wonderful truth that God desires man's fellowship! God desires for man to know and love Him!

Oh! that mere religious men would throw away their garments of self- righteousness - and white collars if need be - and embrace the living reality of a life filled with The Spirit and knowledge of God!

Oh! that unregenerate man, being blinded and dead in spirit, would be free from false suppositions about God and see by The Holy Spirit the person of Jesus and be saved!

Meditation

"Eye has not seen, nor ear heard,
Nor have entered into the heart of man
The things which God has prepared for those who love Him."

1 Corinthians 2:9

DAY 5

"You Must be born again ···born of water and The Spirit"

> *"... Jesus answered, "Most assuredly, I say to you, unless one is **born of water and The Spirit,** he cannot enter the kingdom of God.""*
>
> **John 3: 5**

In this verse of Scripture. Jesus continues to reinforce his answer to Nicodemus. Initially, he told him you must be born again when he said,

> *"Truly, truly I say to you, unless one is born again, he cannot see the Kingdom of God."*

However, Jesus is now saying that you cannot enter the Kingdom of God unless you are born of water and The Spirit. What does Jesus mean by this? Being born of water and The Spirit seems to be moving into more detail about the process of being born again. Jesus is adding the need to be born of water alongside being born of The Holy Spirit. To what does "water" imply or refer? There are numerous answers to this question.

Firstly, we have to think of the time Jesus spoke these words and what this could have meant then instead of what we might think it means today. For example, today, some church ordinances talk of baptism as a necessary sacrament in becoming a Christian which is carried out with babies. However, it is important to realise that this act does not constitute Biblical water baptism since this only has authenticity and meaning to the individual when they reach an age of understanding. Of course, at the time of Jesus, the Church had not yet been birthed to institute this ordinance!

The only acceptable meaning of "water" in this passage has to apply at the time of Jesus, otherwise why say it? Jesus must have been referring to instances and situations at that time where its meaning would be understood.

Several points could fit this situation, including natural birth, which can be described as being *born of water*. Every baby born from the mother's womb breaks through the amniotic fluid that primarily consists of water and is born of "water", signifying a natural birth. It is, therefore, relevant to everyone. In a sense, therefore, there is natural birth, and there is a spiritual birth. One is born of water at birth, and one is born of The Spirit through faith and belief in Christ. Yet, the Scriptures teach us much more than this.

Of John, Jesus said the following words,

> *"Assuredly, I say to you, among those born of women there has not risen one greater than John the Baptist; but he who is least in the kingdom of heaven is greater than he."* **Matthew 11:11**

John the Baptist's appearance was a fulfilment of prophecy.

> *"In those days John the Baptist came preaching in the wilderness of Judea, and saying, "Repent, for the kingdom of heaven is at hand!"*
> *For this is he who was spoken of by the prophet Isaiah, saying,"The voice of one crying in the wilderness: 'Prepare the way of The Lord; Make His paths straight."*
> **Matthew 3: 1-3**

John called people to be baptised in the Jordan river to demonstrate **repentance for their sins,** and Jesus began His public life by submitting Himself to John's baptism. Jesus also started by teaching the people to repent for the Kingdom of Heaven was at hand. Could this be what Jesus was referring to? A pre-requisite to being born again was repentance, and certainly, the baptism of John was well known as a baptism of repentance; this Nicodemus would have understood. The mention of being *born of water* would therefore have brought to mind John's baptism of repentance. Therefore, the ministry of John the Baptist was important in that it prepared the way for Jesus. Its focus underlined the essential need for repentance, which we know is a fundamental requirement for any person to be born again.

The critical and central ingredient of John's baptism was the need to repent of sins. Water baptism, by total immersion, is symbolic of the washing away of sin and the beginning of a new life, and everyone would have understood its meaning at the time of Jesus. It is quite likely that Jesus rephrased His original statement to Nicodemus of *the need to be born again* to that of *being born of water as well as The Spirit*, to give him something he could appreciate. Whilst he had no idea of being born again in itself, Nicodemus knew from John's baptism and Old Testament Scriptures the significance of cleansing by water stipulated by Peter on the Day of Pentecost when the Church was born.

"Peter said to them, "Repent, and let every one of **you be baptized in the name of Jesus Christ for the remission of sins;** *and you shall receive the gift of The Holy Spirit.""*

Acts 2: 38

Notice that, at the birth of the Church, Peter instructs people to be baptised in the name of Jesus Christ. This is because salvation is obtained through faith in Jesus Christ alone and His redeeming blood, yet it can only be appropriated through repentance of sin. On the day of Pentecost, Peter preached the Word of God to the crowd, by the unction of The Holy Spirit, quoting from the Old Testament all the Scriptures that pointed to Jesus Christ and how they had been directly or indirectly responsible for his death! Upon hearing this, the men were pricked in their hearts and cried, "Men and brethren! What shall we do?"

"Therefore, let all the house of Israel know assuredly that God has made this Jesus, whom you crucified, both Lord and Christ." Now when they heard this, they were cut to the heart, and said to Peter and the rest of the apostles, "Men and brethren, what shall we do?"
Then Peter said to them, ***"Repent, and let every one of you be baptized in the name of Jesus Christ for the remission of sins; and you shall receive the gift of The Holy Spirit.""***

Acts 2: 36-38

And so, we see here a culmination of what Jesus, in essence, was speaking to Nicodemus about.

You need to be born again - of water and of The Spirit.

Jesus, Himself, was the sacrifice that provided the cleansing blood for sin, but each person had to be prepared to repent and start a new life in Him too! Hence John the Baptist had gone before Jesus for this very purpose preaching his baptism of repentance.
The purpose of the baptism in water in the name of Jesus Christ was again symbolic. It was a public witness to confirm and demonstrate to the world that the person had repented of their sin, *dying to the old life,* and was now beginning a new life following the teachings of Jesus Christ. So, water baptism in Jesus Christ's name was a declaration of being cleansed from the past life of sin to a new life in Him. The baptism did not save them or contribute to their salvation in Christ, but their repentance and faith in Christ did.

Meditation

*"...Christ also loved the church and gave Himself for her, that He might sanctify and cleanse her with **the washing of water by the word,** that He might present her to Himself a glorious church, not having spot or wrinkle or any such thing, but that she should be holy and without blemish."*
Ephesians 5:25-27

*"Since you have purified your souls in **obeying the truth through The Spirit** in sincere love of the brethren, love one another fervently with a pure heart, **having been born again, not of corruptible seed but incorruptible, through the word of God which lives and abides forever**..."*
1 Peter 1: 22-23

Prayer

I believe that You, Lord Jesus, and You alone have paid the price for my sins upon the cross.
I, therefore, ask You to make me Your child and that I may be born again; that I might be saved and know of a certainty that I shall go to be with You in Heaven when I die.
*I no longer trust my good works, going to church, and doing my best in life to **save me.***
I wish to turn my life around and walk the way You teach and show me from Your Word.
I believe that this is Your free gift to me personally – Eternal Life – and that I shall see the Kingdom of God. Amen

DAY 6

What Does it Mean to Repent?

A word commonly used in the Bible, especially in the New Testament, but hardly ever used, if at all, outside of the church is *repent*. What does the word mean?
First of all, the word *repentance* is the noun whilst the word *repent* is the verb (or action). The Greek word for **repent** means to **think differently**[1]. The Biblical use of the word is extremely important, and our salvation depends upon it! The Scripture below shows us that it is an action that God commands of all men for them to be saved:

> "...*Truly, these times of ignorance God overlooked, but now **commands all men everywhere to repent**, because He has appointed a day on which He will judge the world in righteousness...*"
> **Acts 17:30-31**

Each person needs to think entirely differently about their perspective and outlook in life regarding themselves and God. To be changed through repentance and be born again, we need to hear the Word of God, usually spoken or preached to us at some point upon which our hearts respond and choose to believe and receive it. In this respect, God The Holy Spirit has been sent to work upon the hearts of all people.

> "...I (Jesus) will send Him (The Holy Spirit) to you. And when He has come, He will convict the world of sin, and of righteousness, and of judgement..."
>
> **John 16:8**

Man cannot save himself; he needs the help – howbeit by conviction and persuasion of The Holy Spirit, which is always a battle! So often, man must come to the end of himself before yielding to The Spirit of Grace – such is The Spiritual warfare taking place hidden behind the scenes!

As mentioned, we need to hear the Word of Truth. In this book, we shall see that The Holy Spirit always works and moves in conjunction with the Word of God. If a person is challenged or moved somehow through hearing the Word preached, it is because of The Holy Spirit at work in their heart. The Bible says that through hearing and believing the Word of God, we obtain faith.

> "...so then, faith comes by hearing, and hearing by the word of God."
>
> **Romans 10:17**

If only we could realise just how much The Spirit of God has sought to move in our lives! You see, only God knows whether a person is ready to believe His Word and receive it or reject it. We of ourselves can never tell. At this point, I will pause at the interruption of a verse from famous old hymn that immediately comes to mind:

> *O the love that sought me!*
> *O the blood that bought me*
> *O the grace that brought me to the fold,*
> *Wondrous grace that brought me to the fold!*
> **W. Spencer Walton 1850-1906**

Indeed, I look back at my life wondering how I ever became a follower of Jesus Christ and always have to confess it was because He loved me; He sought me; He paid the price with His own blood to purchase me; it was entirely by His Grace and Grace alone that I am saved!

We are commanded to preach The Gospel to all men everywhere, which is the prime mission for the body of Christ called the *Church*. I am sure that each individual in the world hears the Word many times directly or experiences situations during their lifetime when God speaks into their lives through The Holy Spirit's conviction.

God, however, knows the timeline of each person's life from beginning to end and is aware of that moment when a person will finally believe!

When He sees the soil of our heart is *good ground* for the seed of His Word, that is, our heart has reached the stage of being receptive to receiving and not rejecting Him, God moves by His Holy Spirit upon us, leading us to the place of repentance. In other words, it is my act of being willing to change and to think differently about God that initiates a great miracle in the making! To believe and receive His Word is the key. Furthermore, as I repent, perhaps without realising it, the Person of The Holy Spirit begins working within me to bring about this miraculous change in my heart. Hence to be born again is to be born from above or of The Holy Spirit!

Converted people often testify that they suddenly found that God became real to them. Previously in their life, they knew nothing at all of spiritual things, never having had the desire to know about them, yet, here they are now – a born-again believer in Jesus Christ! God does this sort of thing often! Jesus Himself said,

> "*I have not come to call the righteous,* **but sinners, to repentance.**"
> **Luke 5: 32**

After truly repenting, there is a sudden desire to know more about God's Word, start reading the Bible, and find and fellowship with others who are like-minded.

This book will take us through the amazing pathway of life open to the born-again believer: one who is born from above; one who is born of the incorruptible seed of the Word of God; one who is born of The Holy Spirit; one who has truly repented of their sins and turned their life around to follow Jesus.

The verse below is a reprimand of God to certain people whom He pleads with, night and day, yet they will not believe and repent!

> "...Or do you despise the riches of His goodness, forbearance, and longsuffering, not knowing that **the goodness of God leads you to repentance?"**
>
> **Romans 2:4**

It becomes a great blessing when we realise that it is truly God's goodness that leads us to repentance! It is by God's Grace alone through the atoning blood of Jesus Christ and His death upon the cross that we are led through repentance into eternal life through faith in Jesus alone! When He arose from the dead, Jesus became the means of justifying all sinners who come to God through Him! He has paid the price. Now we must come to Him, repent and be born again.

Observe the reaction of the crowds assembled on the Day of Pentecost after they had heard the Word of God spoken to them by Peter:

> **"Now when they heard this, they were cut to the heart, and said to Peter and the rest of the apostles, "Men and brethren, what shall we do?"**

> *Then Peter said to them, "Repent, and let every one of you be baptized in the name of Jesus Christ for the remission(forgiveness) of sins; and you shall receive the gift of The Holy Spirit. For the promise is to you and to your children, and to all who are afar off, as many as The Lord our God will call."*
>
> **Acts 2: 37-39**

Repentance brings forth a complete change and turn-around in your life. You *turn around and walk in the opposite direction*. Someone once said, "Newly birthed within you is the desire to please God and to walk in newness of life."

It is written,

> *"...therefore, if anyone is in Christ, he is a new creation; old things have passed away; behold, all things have become new."*
>
> **2 Corinthians 5:17**

This desire is directly related to the presence of the new resident within – namely the Person of The Holy Spirit! In conclusion, it is helpful to both see and know that *repentance* is two things. It is an **action** each individual must take by themselves when believing in and receiving Jesus.

Furthermore, it is a **work** of The Spirit of God upon your life so that you become born again of His indwelling Holy Spirit! Simply put, repentance initiates God's grace and all that follows! Remember, this miracle is totally founded upon God's grace and mercy to each believer as a result of the atoning blood of Christ, which alone deems you acceptable to God in Him. It is not because I might be worthy of it by my own good works because the Bible says emphatically,

> *"For by grace, you have been saved through faith, and that not of yourselves; it is the gift of God, not of works, lest anyone should boast."*
> **Ephesians 2: 8-9**

Meditation

Jesus began His ministry by saying,

> ... ***"Repent, for the kingdom of heaven is at hand."***
> **Matthew 4: 17**

Furthermore Reading:

God shows the Apostles that Salvation in Christ through repentance is granted to the Gentiles also and not just the Jews!

Acts 10 – 11:18

"...when they (the Apostles and Brethren in Jerusalem) heard these things (from Peter) they became silent; and they glorified God, saying, **"Then God has also granted to the Gentiles repentance to life.""**

Acts 11: 18

DAY 7

The Flesh

"That which is born of the flesh is flesh, and that which is born of The Spirit is spirit. Do not marvel that I said to you, 'You must be born again.'"

John 3: 6-7

Here Jesus is addressing two things, "the flesh" and "The Spirit" and the difference between them is why a new birth is necessary. In fact, Jesus stresses that we should not be surprised He is saying this! *"Marvel not!"* We shall see that those who are "in the flesh" or "of the flesh" are totally incapable of loving, obeying or knowing God. Man's sinful human nature makes this impossible! To be reunited with God, a person has to have a new nature that is alive to God! This new nature cannot happen through normal means. It requires that a person be "born again" – this time by The Spirit of God!

Consequently, we shall see that New Testament teaching relates the "flesh" and the "spirit" as opposed to one another. We will compare and contrast the vast difference between the two. There is always a conflict between them, and they can never agree! The verse below illustrates this.

> *"There is therefore now no condemnation to those who are in Christ Jesus, **who do not walk according to the flesh, but according to The Spirit.**"*
>
> **Romans 8: 1**

This verse reminds us of *repentance* whereby we turn from the direction we are travelling and walk in the opposite direction! Walking according to The Spirit will indeed be rather like this! Today, we shall concentrate upon those words of Jesus – *"That which is born of the flesh is flesh."*

The Greek word for *flesh* is *sarx* and means the "flesh of the body" instead of the soul or spirit. Therefore, by implication, it refers to the natural man and his human nature. However, in the Scriptures, the word *flesh* is primarily used as a metaphor to describe sinful tendency, so, in such cases, the word *flesh* would refer to man's sinful human nature acquired at birth. Hence the meaning of **Romans 8:1** becomes clearer. God's child is not to walk according to the flesh or the sinful human nature, but The Spirit.

A baby is not taught how to stamp their feet or have a tantrum! They do it naturally! Then, before you know it, they begin to assert themselves with the words *no! why! What's that!* The list increases with age! The beautiful little darling soon becomes knowledgeable, crafty and cute, knowing how to get their own way by displaying fine performances of crocodile tears. Once this works for them, they become like a shark at the smell of blood, going for whatever liberty they can get trying to play up mum and dad as often as they can!

Human nature, as it develops, soon shows what it is capable of, and we need not describe that; it is well known. Human nature is a *fallen nature* from what God originally intended. The theological term is a *degenerate nature*. Hence man needs to be born again into a new life, known as *regeneration*. This new life is not simply a moral or religious reform but the bringing forth of a new life through the work of The Holy Spirit. In other words, to belong to the Heavenly Kingdom, you must be born into it. There is no other way of attaining entry! That is why Jesus said,

> *"That which is born of the flesh is flesh, and that which is born of The Spirit is spirit. Do not marvel that I said to you, 'You must be born again.'"*
>
> **John 3: 6-7**

There are other words widely used in the Bible that we should define to open up the Scriptures with more clarity. For example, the word *flesh* is a metaphor meaning man's sinful human nature acquired at birth. *Carnal* is another word that has the same meaning as *flesh*, referring to man's sinful human nature, passions, and lusts.

Finally, we need to look at the word *lust* used many, many times in the New Testament, so what is its root meaning in Scripture?

The original Greek for *lust(s)* is:

epithumia – a longing desire, especially of that which is forbidden. It is derived from another Greek word, *epithumeo* - to set the heart upon; to long for.

It is important to look at some Scriptures that use the above definitions to help us appreciate a fuller meaning of what is being said! Whilst we do not have to be Greek scholars, we need to extract the truth from key Greek words that appear in the Bible.

> *"For those who live according to the **flesh** set their minds on the things of the **flesh**, but those who live according to The Spirit, the things of The Spirit. For to be **carnally minded** is death, but to be **spiritually minded** is life and peace. Because the **carnal mind** is enmity against God; for it is not subject to the law of God, nor indeed can be. So then, those who are in the **flesh** cannot please God."*
> **Romans 8: 5-8**

The above passage is now clearer to understand and uses the words *flesh* and *carnal* six times. Observe how a person chooses to set their minds upon one of two things – the *flesh* or The Spirit! In tomorrow's meditations, we shall look in detail at what it means to be *Spiritually minded*. However, we can now appreciate that even though we may be born again, we still have the two options always before us – whether to follow the *old man* (*flesh*) or the *new man* created in righteousness.

> *"This I say, therefore, and testify in The Lord, that you should no longer walk as the rest of the Gentiles walk, in the futility of their mind...that you **put off,** concerning your former conduct, the **old man** which grows corrupt according to the deceitful **lusts**, and be renewed in The Spirit of your mind, and that you **put on** the **new man** which was created according to God, in true righteousness and holiness."*
>
> **Ephesians 4: 17, 22-24**

Hence, there will always be a choice in life described here as *putting off* the old and *putting on* the new. You have to make that choice! Remember, If you have already chosen to follow Jesus, it does not end there! Your spiritual life and walk with God are just beginning. Having been born into The Spirit realm where God dwells, you now, rather like a newborn baby who, having left the mother's womb, enters the physical world, enter into a new and totally different world of The Spirit where God reigns; a place where God The Holy Spirit will be real and alive to you. In particular, He will have significant input into your life through the living Word of God by continually helping and directing you to grow in grace and the knowledge of The Lord.

> *"How can a young man cleanse his way?*
> *By taking heed according to Your word."*
>
> **Psalm 119: 9**

Prayer

O Lord! in a sense, I see the future is down to me! I must choose! I cannot abdicate my responsibilities now that I have been saved by Your Grace. And yet I shall never be alone for You have promised to always be with me and never to forsake me!

Lord! I believe You hold my future in Your hands. I choose today to walk with You without fear into it!

You have made Your Word very clear to me today!

Teach me, Lord, and show me Your pathway for my life which I now yield to You.

Part of an old Hymn:

Guide me, O Thou great Jehovah,
Pilgrim through this barren land.
I am weak, but Thou art mighty;
Hold me with Thy powerful hand.

"Guide Me, O Thou Great Jehovah"
William Williams, pub.1745

DAY 8

The Spirit

> *"That which is born of the flesh is flesh, and **that which is born of The Spirit is spirit**. Do not marvel that I said to you, 'You must be born again.'"*
>
> **John 3: 6-7**

A door is now open to us through The Spirit who is called The Spirit of God, The Spirit of the Living God, The Spirit of Christ, The Spirit of Grace, The Holy Spirit and many other names, each one signifying a particular emphasis! Who exactly is He? What is He to the child of God?

The main purpose of writing this book is to answer these questions. We shall see that we are to live in the realm of The Holy Spirit and indeed to live in His power. As newly born-again believers, we need to understand from the Scriptures exactly who we now are in Christ! Furthermore, to see and appreciate the potential we have through our position in Christ and the realm of The Holy Spirit! All of these things are to be brought into fruition through the amazing, miraculous new birth!

It is not some doctrine meant for the scholar to dispute and discuss then to be put aside with little relevance in the life of a believer! We shall vividly see that He, The Spirit of God, has been sent to each believer as a personal companion! The Holy Spirit is mysterious, unfathomable and inexplicable to the natural mind. Yet, He is God, the Third Person of the Trinity, and He becomes very real to the born-again believer forever working in their life daily. Who is He to you? That The Spirit of God, who helped create the universe mentioned in Genesis, abides within each born-again believer is a miraculous state of affairs!

> *"And The Spirit **of God** was hovering over the face of the waters. Then God said..."*
> **Genesis 1: 2-3**

It is He who performed the creative works of God as God spoke the Word, and it was done that is the one who has come to dwell within the child of God!

Nicodemus struggled with the statement asserted emphatically by Jesus, *"You must be born again if you are to see the Kingdom of God."*

It means to be born of The Holy Spirit with His new nature! It means to be born and begin to live in the realm of The Holy Spirit! We shall see that The Holy Spirit has a particular mandate for the child of God, that He has come to give us understanding and illumination of the person of Jesus Christ! Jesus himself said,

> *"...when He, The Spirit of truth, has come, He will guide you into all truth; for ...He will glorify Me... "*

John 16: 13-14

In the above verse, Jesus referred to The Holy Spirit twice as *He!* that is, a Person and not a power or force! In fact, there are many characteristics of The Holy Spirit mentioned in the Bible that we understand to apply to *a person*. Here are a few of them:

- **He has a mind; He helps us and intercedes for us;**

"Likewise, The Spirit also helps in our weaknesses. For we do not know what we should pray for as we ought, **but The Spirit Himself makes intercession for us** *with groanings which cannot be uttered. Now He who searches the hearts knows what* **the mind of The Spirit is***, because He makes intercession for the saints according to the will of God."*
Romans 8: 27

- **He has a will;**

"But one and the same Spirit works all these things, distributing to each one individually as **He wills.***"*
1 Corinthians 12:11

- **He has feelings;**

"And **do not grieve The Holy Spirit** *of God, by whom you were sealed for the day of redemption."*
Ephesians 4:30

To better understand the Person of The Holy Spirit, we need to look at some of the many different names given to Him, each one highlighting an important aspect of who He is. Here are just a few:

- **The Spirit of Christ;**

*"But you are not in the flesh but in The Spirit, if indeed The Spirit of God dwells in you. Now if anyone does not have The Spirit **of Christ,** he is not His. And if Christ is in you, the body is dead because of sin, but The Spirit is life because of righteousness."*
Romans 8: 9-10

- **The Spirit of Grace;**

*"…who has trampled the Son of God underfoot, counted the blood of the covenant by which he was sanctified a common thing, and insulted The Spirit
of grace?"*
Hebrews 10:29

- **The Spirit of Truth;**

*"But when the Helper comes, whom I shall send to you from The Father, The Spirit **of truth** who proceeds from The Father, He will testify of Me."*
John 15:26

- **The Spirit of Power, love and a sound mind;**

> *"For God has not given us a spirit of fear, but of*
> ***power and of love and of a sound mind."***
> **2 Timothy 1:7**

A born-again believer who has read The Bible will undoubtedly have recognised the eternal nature of The Spirit of God who has always co-existed with The Father and the Son. Nevertheless, it is good to include a specific verse to verify this. The following Scripture declares The Spirit of God to be a Person of an eternal nature:

> *"... how much more shall the blood of Christ, who through the **eternal Spirit** offered Himself without spot to God, cleanse your conscience from dead works to serve the living God?"*
> **Hebrews 9: 14**

It was the eternal Spirit of God who inspired men throughout the ages to write down the Scriptures. The authenticity and Divine nature of the Bible as the inspired Word of God are emphatically declared in the Scriptures.

> ***"All Scripture is given by inspiration of God,*** *and is profitable for doctrine, for reproof, for correction, for instruction in righteousness, that the man of God may be complete, thoroughly equipped for every good work."*
> **2 Timothy 3:16-17**

> *"...knowing this first, that no prophecy of Scriptural is of any private interpretation, for **prophecy never came by the will of man**, but holy men of God spoke as they were **moved by The Holy Spirit."***
>
> **2 Peter 1:20-21**

The Word of God always stands true! It will never pass away! Let man be wrong, and always let God be right! Today, this chapter has briefly highlighted some foundational truths about The Holy Spirit using the Bible as the only source. In reality, as well as by reading and teaching of the Scriptures, a born-again child of God will discover much experientially throughout their daily life and walk with God. They will receive confirmations and illuminations by The Spirit of God confirming these Biblical truths as they have personal communion and fellowship with Him!

Prayer

I thank You today, Lord, for the illumination and reality of The Holy Spirit declared in the Scriptures. I desire to walk with You daily, reading Your Word to know and experience this reality in my life continually,

PART 2

New Purpose

DAY 9

The Call of Abraham

> *"Get out of your country, from your family and from your father's house to a land that I will show you. I will make you a great nation. I will bless you and make your name great and you shall be a blessing. I will bless those who bless you, and I will curse him who curses you and in you all the families of the earth shall be blessed."*
>
> **Genesis 12: 1-3**

Did God see in Abraham a man who was different from his surrounding contemporaries? Did He observe a man who would grasp the opportunity to leave all behind him and follow His command? The fact was, Abraham took God at His Word! He obeyed God's direct command, and he is to us a model of obedience and faith. God said of Abraham that because he believed in The Lord,

> *"…He accounted it to him for righteousness."*
> **Genesis 15: 6**

God's call to Abraham rings a familiar note in the New Testament where God says,

> *"Come out from among them*
> *And be separate, says The Lord.*
> *Do not touch what is unclean,*
> *And I will receive you."*
> *"I will be a Father to you,*
> *And you shall be My sons and daughters,*
> *Says The Lord Almighty."*
> **2 Corinthians 6: 17-18**

Abraham was 75 years of age when he left Ur of the Chaldees in Mesopotamia, and the year was approximately 2200 BC. This upheaval in life would surely be a challenge to anyone. Abraham, or Abram, his original name, departed, taking his family and all his possessions in answer to the call of God. He was very rich. His wealth, however, was in the form of many sheep, camels, servants, and so on. Even so, being wealthy would only serve to be an even greater challenge. Life can be very comfortable in such circumstances, and let's face it, if we are comfortable and prospering, why move? Not many in Abraham's circumstances would wish to obey such a calling either then or today! The flesh would be strong in such cases, reminding me of a passage of Scripture.

> *"For you see your calling, brethren, that **not many wise according to the flesh, not many mighty, not many noble, are called.** But God has chosen the foolish things of the world to put to shame the wise, and God has chosen the weak things of the world to put to shame the things which are mighty; and the base things of the world and the things which are despised God has chosen, and the things which are not, to bring to nothing the things that are, that no flesh should glory in His presence."*
>
> **1 Corinthians 1: 26-29**

So, we see that Abraham was an exception! He was one of the *"not many."* Despite being noble and rich in this world's goods, he was still obedient to the call of God! When I was born again as a nineteen-year-old, I was challenged by the words of Jesus when He said,

> ..."*If anyone desires to come after Me, let him deny himself, and take up his cross, and follow Me. For whoever desires to save his life will lose it, but whoever loses his life for My sake will find it. **For what profit is it to a man if he gains the whole world, and loses his own soul?** Or what will a man give in exchange for his soul?"*
>
> **Matthew 16: 24-26**

God, by His Spirit, had spoken directly to me, and I could never forget it. So much so that until this day, every decision I have ever made throughout my life has been influenced by the Word written upon my heart that evening as I sat in a church hall. [1]

Even in a loving relationship through His Son, the reality of knowing God still brings with it a dedicated responsibility to please Him and choose His path for my life. We shall see later on in this book that to believe in Jesus is to obey and follow Him in a relationship whereby He is not just Saviour but also Lord of your life, which entails total surrender, submitting to The Holy Spirit who is able to fashion and change us from glory to glory as we yield ourselves to Him through a process called sanctification.

> ***Sanctification:*** *Sanctification is that renewal of our fallen nature by The Holy Spirit, received through faith in Jesus Christ, whose blood cleanses*
>
> *from all sin, whereby we are not only delivered from the guilt of sin, but are progressively washed from its pollution, saved from its power, and are enabled, through grace, to love God.*

We all can experience times of testing in life, sometimes similar to that of Abraham. Perhaps moving area to where God requires you to be can be a challenge, and, just like Abraham, you are very comfortable right where you are.

If the truth were to be known, you would rather not move at all!

Or, on the contrary, you may desire to move away into a larger property or perhaps change area for the sake of a better-paid job when, once again, if the truth were to be known, God wants you right where you are! The real question is this, would I consult God about this matter and seek His will and approval? There comes a time in your life when you must prove to God your loyalty to Him, which is to be above everything and everyone else. If we are willing to seek first the Kingdom of God, then Jesus has assured us that even material things He will eventually add to our lives when He knows He can trust us.

A life living in The Spirit will entail that I always seek to put God's Kingdom above everything else. I now belong to God; Jesus has purchased me through paying my ransom from sin with His blood; I am not my own, I am bought with a price. Questions we all eventually ask ourselves are these, *"What is my purpose in life and what is God's will for my life?"* [1] See *Appendix 1 - My Testimony*

Abraham was wealthy and prosperous, as mentioned previously, but can material gain make us happy and fulfilled in life? The answer to this question is very simple, without God at the centre of my heart and life, there is a gaping void which no one or nothing else can fill.

Consider the life and circumstances surrounding Abraham and ponder the way he may have felt upon hearing the direct command from God! What was it that compelled him to leave, forsaking all, not knowing his destination? Did Abraham follow The Lord's command believing it would lead to a better life? Did he see that obeying God would be a real purpose and fulfilment in life compared to that which currently occupied him?

Having a purpose is fundamentally important to everyone. Highly qualified and professional people can sometimes abandon their careers and instead opt out to do something more enjoyable and fulfilling, like a city banker becoming a farmer or a scientist choosing to teach children. It is not sufficient for the soul of man to live without a purpose! Abraham saw an objective, a goal before him that challenged him, but it probably appealed to him as well, for God promised to bless him. His wealth was not enough by itself; his heart wanted real direction and purpose, which was his opportunity. What did God actually say to Abraham at the beginning?

> **"Get out of your country**, *from your family and from your father's house to a land that I will show you. I will make you a great nation. I will bless you and make your name great…"*

Furthermore, and perhaps most relevant of all, we should never underestimate the transformation that can take place in our lives the moment we realise God is speaking personally to us! In the final analysis, when God speaks to a person, they instantly recognise the voice of their creator and this above all else is what drives them into an instant change of direction! Abraham experienced just that!

Saul of Tarsus was someone else who had a similar experience whilst journeying on the Damascus road to persecute Christians. Upon hearing the voice of Jesus from Heaven, he immediately thought differently from that time onwards about Jesus Christ. His life instantly changed, for he had a living encounter with the living God.

> *"As he (Saul) journeyed he came near Damascus, and suddenly a light shone around him from heaven. Then he fell to the ground, and heard a voice saying to him,* **"Saul, Saul, why are you persecuting Me?"**
> *And he said,* **"Who are You, Lord?"**
> *Then The Lord said,* **"I am Jesus…**
> *So, Saul, trembling and astonished, said,* **"Lord, what do You want me to do?""**
> **Acts 9: 3-6**

We must remember that God knows how to speak individually to each person and uses different ways as He sees fit. The common factor is that we need to hear God's Word speaking to our hearts bringing about change. When God speaks, miracles happen!

Having obeyed the call of God, Abraham moved forward to other pastures farther afield, not knowing where he was going or how long the journey would last! How great it is to know God's calling in your life! Through trusting in God and being obedient, yielding over to Him the reins of your life, you can learn to walk in peace and great joy.

"He who calls you is faithful, who also will do it."
1 Thessalonians 5:24

Verse and Chorus of an Old Hymn

When we walk with The Lord
In the light of His Word,
What a glory He sheds on our way;
While we do His good will,
He abides with us still,
And with all who will trust and obey.

Trust and obey,
For there's no other way
To be happy in Jesus,
But to trust and obey.

John Henry Sammis (1846-1919)

Verse of an Old Song

I want God's way to be my way,
As I journey here below.
For there is no other highway
That a child of God should go.
Though the road be steep and rough,

*If he leads me it's enough,
I want God's way to be my way every day.*

DAY 10

Abraham's Challenge

We saw on Day 9 that God had commanded Abraham to move from his own country and his father's house. It was significant because on the other side of the river Euphrates in the land of Ur of the Chaldees, including the house of Abraham, they worshiped idols. Having separated Abraham from his homeland and idolatrous family, God planned to make him and his descendants a nation from out of which would come the Messiah!

> *"... I will make you a great nation. I will bless you and make your name great and you shall be a blessing. I will bless those who bless you, and I will curse him who curses you and **in you all the families of the earth shall be blessed.**"*
> **Genesis 12: 2-3**

Joshua said to the people,

> *" ... thus, says The Lord God of Israel, **'Your fathers, including Terah, The Father of Abraham ...dwelt on the other side of the River in old times; and they served other gods.'"***
> **Joshua 24: 2**

Abrahams father was called Terah, and he had two other sons besides Abraham. One was called Haran, who himself had a son named Lot. Haran died whilst in Ur, so when Abraham went out on his journey, he also took his father, Terah, and Lot, his nephew, and Lot's wife. Both Abraham and Lot were wealthy with cattle and many servants, so a large company left together.

Abraham followed the river Euphrates from Ur, which today would be called Southern Iraq, and travelled north-west for approximately 800 miles when he stopped at Haran in Northern Syria. The stay at Haran was probably a long one until Terah, Abraham's father, died at 205 years of age. The Bible says that Abraham was 75 years old when he left Haran, and he still had to travel a furthermore 700 or so miles before reaching the land of Canaan. However, it is clear that God took Terah before Abraham travelled any furthermore. It is possible that God waited to separate Abraham from his idolatrous past so that he was totally free from any family connections of influence that would be contrary to God's plans and purposes.

This serves as a lesson to us today. As a child of God, we are born into the Kingdom of God through the regeneration of The Holy Spirit, and we have become the purchased possession of God, redeemed by the Blood of Jesus from the bondage of sin to serve the Living God! Because of this, our greatest loyalty is to God above all else! God is Holy, and He cannot work in us and through us if we become entangled again in sin. This is no less the case when our family and relationships hinder the way.

> *"Do not be **unequally yoked together with unbelievers.** For what fellowship has righteousness with lawlessness? And what communion has light with darkness?"*
> **2 Corinthians 6:14**

> *"He who loves father or mother more than Me is not worthy of Me. And he who loves son or daughter more than Me is not worthy of Me."*
> **Matthew 10:37**

God does not apologize for requiring His people to put Him first in all things, which becomes clear once we accept and realise that God's purposes for our lives, rather like those of Abraham, are just that – His purposes! He directs our lives now through our obedience and submission to His Word and has full authority to do so.

Whilst God requires this of us; He does not force the issue. God never overrules freedom of choice. Instead, He gives us a new heart through being born again of His Holy Spirit so that through His love and personal communion, we can establish together a relationship with Him whereby we then learn to trust God and obey Him. God works in this way by His Grace towards us in Christ Jesus. He gradually draws us into His plans for our lives by perfecting our ways, mainly through His Word.

The children of Israel were, at one time, given over by God to be taken captive into Babylon by Nebuchadnezzar because of their unrepentant stubbornness in refusing to turn away from idolatry and rebellion even though Jeremiah the prophet had warned them for several decades before. God said they would be taken into captivity for seventy years if they did not repent. The outcome was this; they were taken into captivity! Even so, God honoured His covenant with them when he sent word to those in captivity by saying,

"For thus says The Lord: After seventy years are completed at Babylon, I will visit you and perform My good word toward you, and cause you to return to this place. **For I know the thoughts that I think toward you, says The Lord, thoughts of peace and not of evil, to give you a future and a hope."*
Jeremiah 29: 10-11

If you were to read the whole Book of Jeremiah, you would soon discover God's abhorrence and revulsion in dealing with His people! The above passage serves to remind us that whilst His people may have given up on God and turned away from Him, God never gave up upon them, truly illuminating God's love towards us! It is not a wishy-washy tolerance that sees and ignores our sin under the false assertion that "God is love!" Rather, God will chastise and convict us of our sin and, if necessary, leave us for a while to our own devices until we ultimately come to our senses and turn to Him.

Abraham eventually reaches the land of Canaan and no sooner does he arrive when a great challenge confronts him. There is a famine in the land, but nearby Egypt had plenty of food. Consequently, Abraham ventures down into Egypt, planning to deceive Pharaoh, fearing that he would observe and desire his beautiful wife, Sarah, and kill him in the process. Consequently, Abraham told his wife to tell the people that she was his sister! Abraham said to Sarah these words,

> "Therefore, it will happen, when the Egyptians see you, that they will say, 'This is his wife'; and they will kill me, but they will let you live. Please say you are my sister, that it may be well with me for your sake, and that I may live because of you."
> **Genesis 12: 12-13**

Abraham had anticipated correctly, for Pharaoh did enquire about Sarah, and the plan of deception was set in motion when she lied, saying she was Abraham's sister. The outcome was that God plagued Pharaoh and his house with great plagues because of Sarah, Abraham's wife.

> "And Pharaoh called Abram and said, "What is this you have done to me? Why did you not tell me that she was your wife? Why did you say, 'She is my sister'? I might have taken her as my wife. Now therefore, here is your wife; take her and go your way.""
> **Genesis 12: 18**

After this escapade, Abraham left with his wife and all that he had, and the Bible says that he journeyed back to Bethel, where he had previously set up camp, which serves as a significant lesson to us today! Let us discover and realize from Abraham's actions what we should do when we falter, just as Abraham had done.

When he first entered the promised land of Canaan, Abraham had built an altar and called upon The Lord's name between Bethel and Ai. After leaving Egypt, Abraham journeyed straight back to the place he had left before becoming entangled with the Egyptians, back to Bethel, where he once again calls upon the name of The Lord at the very same altar he had previously built. We should follow this pattern of behaviour if our hearts condemn us because of faltering along the way! If we have sinned or perhaps made a wrong choice without consulting The Lord and we are now remorseful, feeling we have failed, let us return to The Lord. In this passage of Scripture, we are shown, by the example of Abraham, to go straight back to where we left off following The Lord and repent before Him establishing our walk and relationship with God once again. Abraham turned (repentance) and went to an altar - a memorial he had built because it was here that God had spoken to him.

It served as a permanent reminder of when he had previously given thanks to God and where he had prayed before Him in gratitude and reverence! Let us, therefore, be willing to go back to our *altar of The Lord*, that is, the place called *Calvary*, our *Bethel*, and kneel before *the cross* where Jesus died for our sins.

Let us, like Abraham, turn back to the place where we knew the voice of The Lord before we erred and call upon the Name of The Lord in repentance.

We all falter at some time or another! Abraham faced up to the fact that he had done wrong. He didn't try to hide his experience in Egypt or forget it. No! Abraham's conscience was such that he felt compelled to face up to his actions before God and to get right with God. he returned straight to Bethel, where he had left off on his way towards Egypt and addressed the issue by getting before God upon his knees! God did not choose Abraham because his character and integrity were exemplary but because he believed God and obeyed His word and directive.

Faith simply takes God at His Word, and this was a quality Abraham possessed. By his faith, Abraham became the model of faith for the believer. Let us never underestimate the fact that believing God is foundational to our faith and Salvation! It is essential if we are to have a personal relationship with God

"Can two walk together, unless they are agreed?"
Amos 3:3

Prayer

Thank You, Lord, that I can turn to You whenever I have departed from Your Way. The blood of Jesus shed for all my sin means You promise to receive me and forgive me.

Thank You; I can now see that believing in You means I trust You by faith, which entails trusting and keeping Your Word. Strengthen me with Your power and strength.

Meditation

"Come now, and let us reason together,"
Says The Lord,"Though your sins are like scarlet,
They shall be as white as snow;
Though they are red like crimson,
They shall be as wool."

Day 11

Choices and Decisions

Life-changing decisions can come upon us without notice or expectation. Should we change jobs and move to another area? If so, what impact would this have upon our children changing school and our church where we teach in Sunday School, enjoy great fellowship, and hear the rare, good, sound Word of God preached and taught? The usual dilemma is whether such a move is God's will, and the outcome can be a sensitive one.

The real question is, "Am I happy to stay or go wherever God leads me? Am I thinking of moving into a place where God is still paramount in my life, or is it that the appeal of the flesh is very great?" A better house and job can be tempting and would perhaps not serve as a real problem or issue to anyone other than a child of God. If we have chosen to serve Him first above all else, then there is only one solution – pray.

My wife and I were in the same position in the early years of our marriage whilst living in two rooms in London with one baby. Everything made sense outwardly! We needed larger accommodation, and we certainly could not afford to buy a house in London. Furthermore, family and friends, who lived 150 miles away, made it very clear that living in London was not the best place to bring up a family and suggested we move into the countryside where houses were cheaper.

After much prayer, we knew God wanted us to stay in London! We were attending a Bible-teaching church and needed to be grounded in God's Word. We both taught in Sunday School, and I had become an elder and occasionally preached. We also did teens work mid-week...! Our decision to stay made it difficult to think too much about the church and not enough about ourselves and our family! Whilst we understood their feelings, the decision had to be ours! It was very tough, yet despite all this, we experienced great peace and joy knowing we were serving The Lord and were in His will. We could not disobey God, not even for the sake of family. We were fully assured in our hearts that God knew what was best for us in the long term! The following is a verse of a favourite hymn of ours during this time.

I'd rather have Jesus than silver or gold;
I'd rather be His than have riches untold;
I'd rather have Jesus than houses or lands.
I'd rather be led by His nail pierced hand

Chorus:
Than to be the king of a vast domain
Or be held in sin's dread sway.
I'd rather have Jesus than anything
This world affords today.

Written in 1922 by Rhea F. Miller with the music composed by George Beverly Shea.

The fact is, decisions and choices form a significant part in our life determining the direction we take. Therefore, we do well to remember and realise that only God knows what will work for us and what will not, what will make us happy and fulfilled and what will not. Therefore, it is always wise to seek first God's Kingdom regarding a matter and allow God to lead by yielding to His purposes and plans. I would rather be in the will of God, whatever the outcome! God had spoken to me at the very beginning of my walk with Him with a challenging word that changed me forever:

> *"If anyone desires to come after Me, let him deny himself, and take up his cross, and follow Me. For whoever desires to save his life will lose it, but whoever loses his life for My sake will find it. For what profit is it to a man if he gains the whole world, and loses his own soul? Or what will a man give in exchange for his soul?"*
> **Matthew 16: 24-26**

A child of God, born of His Spirit, still possesses a free will so, God, in His love and mercy, calls us to surrender all by submitting our lives to Him. Being born again is just the beginning; we must follow on to know The Lord by allowing the Word of God to change us!

> *"I beseech you, therefore, brethren, by the mercies of God, that you present your bodies a living sacrifice, holy, acceptable to God, which is your reasonable service. And do not be conformed to this world, but be transformed by the renewing of your mind, that you may prove what is that good and acceptable and perfect will of God."*
> **Romans 12:1-2**

To know God's calling upon your life, you will need to know God's Word, so, from the very beginning of your walk with God, you need to be taught God's Word as it is written, unadulterated, and verse by verse! God knows our future, and He desires to bless us by leading us along His pathway, but we need to get to know Him. God is our guide, teacher, and counsellor. As we read and meditate upon His Word regularly, we will learn of God's ways and God's thoughts about life!

It was at the age of nineteen years when I had come to The Lord that I had this insatiable longing within my heart! I wanted God to be real, to speak to Him, and to hear from Him. As I read God's Word, I called upon Him for help and guidance. Knowing very little, I asked a Bible student if he knew a Scripture about guidance, and this is what he gave me:

> *"I will instruct you and teach you in the way you should go; I will guide you with My eye."*
> **Psalm 32:8**

I clung on to this verse, and indeed the whole chapter. It was just what I needed. God had promised to instruct me and guide me, so I asked of Him. He said He would guide me with His eye! (Years later, I realized this was referring to God's Counsel but what I saw was God looking down upon me.) Sure enough, God finds a way of speaking to you through His Word and by His Holy Spirit. Thus, God opened a door for me to enter Furthermore Education as a lecturer. I met and taught lots of students from all parts of the world, providing me with ripe harvest fields and the opportunity to minister to many people. It lasted 37 years!

It was a simple faith, taking God at His Word, which opened things up to me in a big way! I read wonderful things in the Word, such as being made alive out of darkness into His marvellous Light! Dwelling in the realm of The Spirit, in the Light and Kingdom of God, became a living reality to me

> *"But you are a chosen generation, a royal priesthood, a holy nation, His own special people, that you may proclaim the praises of Him who called you out of darkness into His marvellous light."*
> **1Peter2:9**

> *"He has delivered us from the power of darkness and translated (conveyed) us into the kingdom of the Son of His love, in whom we have redemption through His blood, the forgiveness of sins."*
> **Colossians 1:13-14**

The reality of knowing God can only come about through understanding His Word illuminated by The Spirit of God and His presence within. The Word of God infused with The Spirit of God and received into your life is dynamite!

Upon reflection, I believe the following pointers helped me:

- *Die completely to self.*
- *Yield yourself unconditionally to do God's will for your life!*
- *God is a humble person, so – humble yourself!*
- *God is all-knowing, so - trust Him!*
- *God is Holy and righteous, so – believe and follow Him!*
- *God is reliable and true to His Word, so- learn of Him and keep His Word in your heart.*

Notice how the above are all choices that we must make! Things don't happen by themselves! However, our choices will be determined by our outlook in life and whether it is Christ-centred or self-centred! This is the crunch for everyone, and it is no respecter of persons! Remember Lot's choice?

Furthermore, do you desire to know what God has planned for you in your life? Well, some years ago, I discovered an amazing truth from the Scriptures. Did you know that God has imparted within each of His children specific gifts, talents, and works unique to each of us!?

> *"For we are His workmanship, created in Christ Jesus for good works, which God prepared, beforehand that we should walk in them."*
> **Ephesians 2:10**

What good news for every child of God! These works mentioned above are not part of our Salvation neither do they contribute to it. We can only be saved through faith in Jesus Christ and His shed Blood for us, but the truth is, God knew us before the world began and that we would be alive here on Earth at this time. He sees the end from the beginning - and that's considering all our free will choices - so He certainly knows your timeline. He has created each one of us uniquely. Just as snowflakes from the sky and our hands' fingerprints are unique, so it is with people; each person is unique! He has given us talents and abilities to use for His glory. God's priority will always be to direct us into these good works both for our pleasure and His, to fulfil His purposes for the Kingdom of God!

There is a spiritual guide within every born-again believer, The Holy Spirit, who shows us the way to go. As we commit our life and decisions to The Lord, He will direct our path.

I used to imagine my life in a similar way to that of Moses and the children of Israel as they were being led out of Egypt into the wilderness towards the promised land.

They would be guided by a pillar of cloud by day and a pillar of fire by night. When the pillar stopped, they also stopped and set up camp. If the pillar began to move then, it was time to pack up and leave. If the pillar of cloud remained then, they remained! While travelling through the wilderness, Moses wanted assurance from God that He would be with him as he led the children of Israel whom God had called stiff-necked people! They would face enemies who would not respect them and come to places with more than one path to take, so which direction should they go? Taking the wrong path could lead them straight into danger. Consequently, Moses spoke boldly to God, saying,

> *"...then he (Moses) said to Him, (The Lord)*
> *"If Your Presence does not go with us, do not bring us up from here..."*
> **Exodus 33:15**

In other words, Moses wanted to move forward only if God went before them – which is fair enough! Desiring to do God's will is the first step towards achieving it! Moses wanted God's assurance; he asked for it, and he got it! God will always help us when we earnestly desire Him to work in our lives and teach us His way when we choose to follow and keep His Word, asking His help in the process. The Bible says we are pilgrims and sojourners in this world. Are you living your life entirely for God's purposes and serving Him? What a calling! What a blessing! What an eternal hope in seeing Jesus Christ one day to receive a reward which He has promised to give us at His coming.

Remember!

He is there!
He always will be there for us!
Will we be just as faithful?

Prayer

Thank You, Lord that You chose me from the beginning to love You, know You, and serve You until the end – and then to live with You!
Thank You for Your Grace by which I am saved.
Thank You, Jesus, for coming to this Earth and dying upon a cross for my sins. I decide today to choose Your way as my way.

Meditation

Let your focus in life be centred upon the person of Jesus Christ.

DAY 12

The Flesh and The Spirit

On DAY 7, titled *The Flesh*, we saw that *the flesh* refers to man's sinful human nature, passions and lusts. Another word with the same meaning as *the flesh* is the word *carnal*. New Testament teaching relates the "flesh" and the "spirit" in total opposition to one another. When two people are said to be very much alike, we often say they are *two peas from the same pod!* Similarly, when two people are completely different from one another, we say they are *poles apart!* So, it is, according to the latter, between the flesh and The Spirit; they are *poles apart,* and it is impossible to reconcile them.

An interesting statement is found in an area of the Bible that we may not read often, and yet it hits the nail upon the head.

> " Who can bring a clean thing out of an unclean? No one!"
>
> **Job 14:4**

Man was created with a soul of a spiritual nature but being separated from God; his spirit was dead! Through pollution of sin, man's soul is defiled and totally under the power and influence of the lusts of the flesh. The following Scripture renders man's spirit dead to the things of The Spirit of God.

> *"For the flesh lusts against The Spirit, and The Spirit against the flesh; and these are contrary to one another, so that you do not do the things that you wish."*
> **Galatians 5:17**

Once man's unregenerate nature is regenerated (renewed or restored) by The Spirit of God, he becomes a *Spiritual man*. in essence, this is what Jesus was communicating with Nicodemus (day 7) when He said,

> *"That which is born of the flesh is flesh, and that which is born of The Spirit is spirit.* **Do not marvel that I said to you, 'You must be born again.'"**
> **John 3: 6-7**

Therefore, the conclusion of the whole matter is, man, who is by nature a fallen, unregenerate being, needs to be born again of The Spirit of God and made spiritually alive unto God! Make no mistake, those who are in the flesh are dead to the Living God and therefore cannot love, obey, or know Him. Some people attempt to become good enough through self-denial living a life separate from society and all its temptations.

The problem here is looking to ourselves and not looking to God to save us from our sin. As Job said, *"who can bring a clean thing out of an unclean?"*
All our human effort to save ourselves from the penalty of sin are futile. They are the product of a self-righteous attitude that affirms *I can make myself right or at least be good enough and surely God will accept that?!* Such a person underestimates the depravity of embedded sin within their fallen human nature as well as denying the Word of God that affirms God alone can save us from our plight:

> *"...if we walk in the light as He is in the light, we have fellowship with one another, and the blood of Jesus Christ His Son cleanses us from all sin. If we say that we have no sin, we deceive ourselves, and the truth is not in us.* **If we confess our sins, He is faithful and just to forgive us our sins and to cleanse us from all unrighteousness.** *If we say that we have not sinned, we make Him a liar, and His word is not in us."*
>
> **1 John 1: 7-10**

It is often said that man is a sinner because he sins, whereas it would be more accurate to say man sins because he is a sinner! We need to understand this; we are all born with a sinful human nature, and there is nothing man can do about it, except, that is, receive the cleansing of the blood of Jesus, which alone can wash away your sin.

> *"Who can say,* **'I have made my heart clean, I am pure from my sin?'"**
>
> **Proverbs 20:9**

The Bible says God made man a spirit, soul and body, and his spirit is dead! We are all dead in our unregenerate state from birth, dead in trespasses and sin. So, first and foremost, we need someone to resurrect our spirit! Jesus does just that.

> *"And you He made alive, who were **dead in trespasses and sins...**"*
> **Ephesians 2:1**

It is possible for people to be interested in "religion" or study the Bible as a mere book and even use it as a profession! We must never automatically assume such are true believers and born-again children of God simply because of the nature of their profession. Neither should we be wooed because of their qualifications, position, grandeur, and prestige. Yes, it is possible for a person to obtain a Ph.D. in theology or be the Principal of a Bible College and not be saved from their sin! Remember Nicodemus was of profound religious standing and a member of the Sanhedrin? I remember my Religious Studies teacher at school saying he did not believe in the miracles of Jesus and considered them as mere stories! That's how it can be!

We have clearly seen from the Scriptures what they teach us! Jesus said a person *must be born-again,* if they are to see the Kingdom of God!

It is essential to realise that man cannot save himself by his good deeds and religious life.

We should never be a respecter of persons simply because of any worldly status, importance or qualifications as they have no bearing whatsoever on one's spiritual state before God! Becoming righteous before God is not something man can ever achieve of himself; it is a work of God. God will attribute righteousness, however, to those who believe Him and obey His Word! Remember Abraham?

To be re-united with God, a person must have their nature changed, which cannot happen through normal means. The change has to come about from within by the regenerating power of The Holy Spirit at the new birth, that is, when a person, having repented of their sin, believes upon and receives Jesus Christ has their own personal Lord and Saviour. Also, we should realise that the new life received from God is not some moral or religious reform but the bringing in of a totally New Life in Christ. Indeed, this new birth is a miracle whereby God The Holy Spirit comes to abide in us – yes! God does just that!

The Bible is very clear about the above, yet so many people are unaware of it! Probably this ignorance is because many are not taught the need to be born-again according to the Scriptures. You see, The Holy Spirit literally comes to dwell within you when you become born again!

Once The Holy Spirit takes up residence within us, we become God's possession redeemed by the blood of The Lamb. Yes! It is true! We belong to God! We become His purchased possession; we are not our own! God has hallmarked each of His children by His Holy Spirit coming to live and dwell within them!

Here are some Scriptures that tell us this fact:

*"To them God willed to make known what are the riches of the glory of this mystery among the Gentiles: which is **Christ in you, the hope of glory.**"*
Colossians 1:27

*"...do you not know that **your body is the temple of The Holy Spirit who is in you, whom you have from God, and you are not your own? For you were bought at a price;** therefore, glorify God in your body and in your spirit, **which are God's.**"*
1 Corinthians 6: 19-20

Hence there becomes an interesting situation in the life of a new believer in Christ! He has, residing within him, his old nature of flesh and, at the same time, the new nature of The Spirit, given to him by God! Therefore, how does he move forward with two different and, as we have seen, opposing natures?
As a newborn child of God, we are required in the Scriptures to yield our lives to reading and knowing God's Word seeking to walk in God's way by submitting ourselves to Him every day! Every child of God will immediately gain spiritual understanding through reading the Scriptures. The Holy Spirit will speak to our innermost being and reveal to us the truth about God, His ways and His thoughts, in fact, every single aspect of our life! Jesus said so much about the necessity and benefits of reading and applying God's Word to our personal life, which we will see later.

Consequently, God calls His newborn children to live after The Spirit renouncing the desires of the flesh. Yes, they have been born again; yes, they have been saved, but now they must allow God through His Word to *save them day by day,* teaching them how to walk in The Spirit, being obedient to His Word, and not fulfilling the lust of the flesh. It is a process of growing in the Grace and knowledge of The Lord and will last until Jesus comes again! Then, He will take them to Heaven, and they will finally *be saved* from the very presence of sin!

Finally, in **Romans chapter 8,** we discover much about the conflict between the flesh and The Spirit. We see that:

To walk according to the flesh is to follow the sinful desires of one's old life, whereas, **to walk according to The Spirit is to follow the desires of The Holy Spirit, to live in a way pleasing to Him.**

"There is therefore now no condemnation to those who are in Christ Jesus, **who do not walk according to the flesh, but according to The Spirit."**

Romans 8:1

"For those who live according to the flesh set their **minds** *on the things of the flesh, but those* **who live according to The Spirit, the things of The Spirit"**

Romans 8:5

Below is a wonderful hymn that is still sung today, howbeit, with differing musical arrangements:

What can wash away my sin?
Nothing but the blood of Jesus;
What can make me whole again?
Nothing but the blood of Jesus.
Oh! precious is the flow
That makes me white as snow;
No other fount I know,
Nothing but the blood of Jesus.

For my cleansing this I see —
Nothing but the blood of Jesus!
For my pardon this my plea —
Nothing but the blood of Jesus!

Nothing can my sin erase
Nothing but the blood of Jesus!
Naught of works, 'tis all of grace —
Nothing but the blood of Jesus!

Lyrics and Music: Robert Lowry (1826-1899)

Meditation

"Come now, and let us reason together,"
Says The Lord,"Though your sins are like scarlet,
They shall be as white as snow;
Though they are red like crimson,
They shall be as wool.
Isaiah 1:18

DAY 13

Abraham and Lot

Abraham was already a very rich man when he left Ur of the Chaldees with his nephew Lot. Their journey took them to Haran, where they stayed a good while, and it was here that Terah, Abraham's father died. As they left Haran on their journey to Canaan, the Bible says that Abraham and Lot took even more possessions and servants from Haran.

> *"Then Abram took Sarai his wife and Lot his brother's son,* **and all their possessions that they had gathered, and the people whom they had acquired in Haran***, and they departed to go to the land of Canaan."*
> **Genesis 12:5**

As we saw on DAY 10, Abraham entered Egypt because there was a famine in the land and, in so doing, acted unwisely! By lying about his wife to Pharaoh, saying she was his sister, Abraham caused trouble for himself! Eventually, God saved the day, and when Pharaoh discovered the truth, he sent Abraham away out of Egypt, taking with him even more riches of livestock, silver, and gold!

> *"Then Abram went up from Egypt, he and his wife and all that he had, and Lot with him, to the South. **Abram was very rich in livestock, in silver, and in gold.**"*
> **Genesis 13:1-2**

It was clear that God was blessing Abraham with material wealth, even though that could bring temptations and distractions to doing the will of God. It was Jesus who said,

> *"How hard it is for those who **have riches** to enter the kingdom of God!" And the disciples were astonished at His words. But Jesus answered again and said to them, "Children, how hard it is for those who **trust in riches** to enter the kingdom of God! It is easier for a camel to go through the eye of a needle than for a rich man to enter the kingdom of God."*
> **Mark 10:23-25**

Notice that Jesus clarified the situation by declaring that the difficulty was not being rich but rather what lay in the hearts of those who *trust in riches*.
It is quite clear that God blessed Abraham with riches knowing full well where his heart lay! God can trust some people with wealth, for He knows they will be generous and bless others. In doing so, they will receive furthermore blessing, for *it is more blessed to give than to receive!*

However, by having riches and many possessions, there can be a long list of distractions, selfish commitments, and numerous time-consuming occupations that can drain a person's life from ever possibly serving God or doing His will. Furthermore, wealth can breed a false sense of self-sufficiency and pride when the truth is, only God can satisfy our soul with the true riches of His Grace. That's the way it is! The more money I have, the more I shop, and the more I buy, the more I will become preoccupied and entangled with things. The real danger is that life becomes consumed with unnecessary *possessions* that will all pass away! Ironically, trusting in wealth as the main goal in life only leads to debt, for the more you have, the more you desire! Dissatisfaction and unhappiness are not far behind! You see, any of these material things cannot feed man's spirit! Did not Jesus say,

> *"Man shall not live by bread alone but by every Word of God?"*
>
> **Luke 4:4**

Although Abraham had many riches, he did not trust in them, as we shall see. Therefore, his attitude and heart were not centred upon them, but instead, he sought to follow God's purpose and plan for his life.
Jesus spoke again, warning us of gathering many possessions upon this Earth, far more than we need knowing very well that we would be diverted from the real purpose and calling in life.

> *"Do not lay up for yourselves treasures on earth, where moth and rust destroy and*

where thieves break in and steal; but lay up for yourselves treasures in heaven, where neither moth nor rust destroys and where thieves do not break in and steal. **For where your treasure is, there your heart will be also."**

Matthew 6:19-21

"And He (Jesus) said to them, "Take heed and beware of covetousness, ***for one's life does not consist in the abundance of the things he possesses."***

Luke 12:15

One problem did arise, however, for both Lot and Abraham as they travelled together. The sheer quantity of livestock and people in the two camps were too many for the land to support, causing strife between their herdsmen. During this time, we can observe the character and integrity of Abraham as he faces this challenge within the family. How did he react? Firstly, we see that Abraham highly respected family ties.

"So, Abram said to Lot, "Please let there be no strife between you and me, and between my herdsmen and your herdsmen; for we are brethren."

Genesis 13:8

Abraham was gracious, speaking in this manner to Lot! He cuts off the opportunity for contention, and a potential evil is diffused and ceases! Yet, there is an even greater revelation Abraham's heart following on from his plea to Lot when he said,

> *"Is not the whole land before you? Please separate from me. If you take the left, then I will go to the right; or, if you go to the right, then I will go to the left."*
>
> **Genesis 13:9**

What does this attitude and frame of mind tell you about Abraham? Abraham must have been aware of the greater prospects in the land over by the Jordan River. It was fertile and far superior to any other. Had he been selfish and materially-minded, Abraham would have refrained from making such a proposition to Lot, but we see that wealth and prosperity were not his prime objective in life. Yes, Abraham was rich, but the prospect of becoming even more so did not divert him. His heart was elsewhere!

The good land in question was very fertile, and the only other alternative was, by all standards, a poor substitute in comparison, for there was nothing but desert for miles around! Either Abraham or Lot had to have the dry, barren desert! Who was it to be? The plan was to split up and part company, and Abraham, for the sake of peace and harmony, gave up his right to choose to give this honour to Lot instead. So, wherever Lot desired to go, he was free to do so! Abraham was willing to sacrifice the seemingly better choice of land by allowing Lot to choose first, and this purely to end all strife between them.

Very few, if any, would unselfishly do such a thing given what was at stake. Abrahams actions reveal much about why God chose Abraham in the first place. He was not selfish and desired God's will and purpose over wealth. Whoever possessed the rich plains of the Jordan would surely become even more prosperous, and life would be easier, more comfortable, and more convenient. Previously having accepted the nomadic lifestyle of his uncle to witness God's promise, the challenge and opportunity before him suddenly superceded all such spiritual aspirations that he may have had at the beginning, and he could not resist it! The flesh proved greater than The Spirit! Lot would be better off if he chose this land and he knew it! His future, so he thought, would be very promising; all would be his and his alone with no one else to share it with! Well, after all, is not this the way of the world that we should always seek opportunities to better ourselves!? Abraham was very different indeed! He did not think like that! Neither do those who genuinely desire to walk with God. As it was written previously on DAY 12,

> *"For those who live according to the flesh set their minds on the things of the flesh, but those who live according to The Spirit, the things of The Spirit."*
> **Romans 8:5**

Now we observe the character of Lot as it is revealed to us by his choice, and we observe the things that influenced him.

> **"And Lot lifted his eyes** and saw all the plain of Jordan, that it was well watered everywhere …like the garden of The Lord, like the land of Egypt as you go toward Zoar.
> **Then Lot chose for himself all the plain of Jordan,** and Lot journeyed east. And they separated from each other. Abram dwelt in the land of Canaan, and Lot dwelt in the cities of the plain and pitched his tent even as far as **Sodom. But the men of Sodom were exceedingly wicked and sinful against The Lord."**
> **Genesis 13:10-13**

All that glitters is not gold!

The picture that comes to mind is of Adam and Eve in the Garden of Eden as they beheld the fruit of the tree of the knowledge of good and evil and desired it!

> "So, when the woman **saw that the tree was good for food, that it was pleasant to the eyes,** and a tree desirable to make one wise, she took of its fruit and ate."
> **Genesis 3:6**

How appearances can deceive! Similarly, Lot was to find out the hard way by the choice he had just made!

How often are we short-sighted in moving to a new area only to regret the decision later! Our high expectations can be deceptive and based purely upon outward appearances and an illusion of pleasure and happiness! So often a new house, for example, can be utterly spoilt by one thing - bad neighbours! Lot was about to find out about bad neighbours, for nearby, in the vicinity of his new home, was bad news! As mentioned in the passage of Scripture below.

> *"...Lot dwelt in the cities of the plain and **pitched his tent even as far as Sodom. But the men of Sodom were exceedingly wicked and sinful against The Lord.**"*

As they faced the plains of Jordan, it was here that a test and a challenge arose. What would you do in Lot's position if you knew nothing about what lay ahead? This is the point, is it not? We do not know the future and whether things will work out as God's will for our life or otherwise, hence the need to pray and not make a hasty decision.

I like the words of Moses in the wilderness when he said to The Lord,

> *"**If Your Presence does not go with us, do not bring us up from here.**"*
> **Exodus 33:15**

Not one of us is exempt from the temptations of the flesh; it is what we do about them that matters in the end. Even as born-again believers, we can easily choose to do the wrong thing through yielding to temptation, selfishness, convenience, or desiring an easier life! As we shall see later in this book, we constantly need to live and walk according to The Spirit and crucify, where necessary, the lusts of the flesh! After all, what would it profit us if we gained the whole world's treasures and yet found ourselves lost and far from God?

It is said of Moses:

> "By faith Moses, when he became of age, refused to be called the son of Pharaoh's daughter, **choosing rather to suffer affliction with the people of God than to enjoy the passing pleasures of sin esteeming the reproach of Christ greater riches than the treasures in Egypt."**
> **Hebrews 11:24-26**

We must fear disobeying God or ever moving out of His perfect will for our lives! Lot was unlike his uncle Abraham who was steadfast in purpose and believed that God's promises were greater than all the riches and conveniences this world could offer!

Lot gazed down towards the green valley below, feeling the cool breeze upon his cheeks and a different smell of fresh, lush green grass. It must have seemed like the Garden of Eden! In moments like these, the child of God should examine the situation more closely and, as mentioned previously, pray about any future decision first realising that, despite appearances, it may not be in the will of God. Lot should have prayed and asked God to direct him in his choice, but he clearly chose for himself.

I have found that, in practice, it is God who moves you into a new place when necessary. Remember the pillar of cloud by day and the pillar of fire by night? Where it stayed, the Israelites stayed; when it moved, they followed! If you move by your own accord without God's guidance or if you stay when the pillar has moved on, you will end up in trouble by being in the wrong place!

In the book of Genesis in the Old Testament of the Bible, this incident, between Abraham and Lot, vividly and practically portrays some of the most foundational truths and patterns of behaviour that are so relevant to the life of every born-again believer! They span much of our entire walk with and our attitude towards God!

Meditations

"There is a way that seems right to a man, But its end is the way of death."

Proverbs 14:12

*"Do not be wise in your own eyes;
Fear The Lord and depart from evil."*
Proverbs 3:7

Prayer

Lord teach me to be still and know always that You are God!

I commit my way to You. You know what is best for me, where I work or live.

Let me be content to be in the place You want me to be.

Thought

"I would rather be a doorkeeper in the house of my God Than dwell in the tents of wickedness."
Psalms 84:10

DAY 14

PART 3

Learning to Walk with God

"Can two walk together unless they are agreed?"
Amos 3:3

Denying Yourself

Our understanding of what is meant by "denying yourself" is paramount. The Way Jesus came into this world was to deny Himself and devote His life entirely to doing the will of The Father; this is the pathway for us when we are born again into God's Kingdom. His Way is to be our way. Denying Himself was the path of life He took, and it is the same path we are also called to take. Here is the real challenge for every believer. Jesus said,

> "If anyone desires to come after Me, let him **deny himself,** and take up his cross, and follow Me."
> **Matthew 16:24**

What does this mean from a practical perspective? First of all, it doesn't mean denying ourselves through practicing any form of asceticism. On the contrary, an ascetic deliberately suffers pain, abstains, or becomes reclusive, thinking that this will lead to some form of higher holiness! Indeed, all world religions practise this in some form or another!

That *a person can attain a higher spiritual and moral state by practicing self-denial, self-mortification,* and the like, is not the meaning of "denying oneself" as mentioned by Jesus. Asceticism can never be true. It would undermine and contradict the cleansing power of the Blood of The Lamb, which alone is all-sufficient to makes us holy and acceptable before God without works. Rather, Scripturally denying oneself is more to do with my willingness to accept the following:

> *We should put the interests of God's Kingdom first and foremost in our life above and beyond our own plans.*

We should renounce self-centred ambition even if it is most inconvenient to do so! We must take up *"our cross."* Such sacrifices will result in true joy and fulfilment, experiencing the fullness of Kingdom Life upon earth! Jesus continued,

> *"...For whoever desires to save his life will lose it, but whoever loses his life for My sake will find it..."*
>
> **Matthew 16:25**

By yielding our whole life to the plans and purposes of God, we **find** true Life! If we think we know better and seek to do "our own thing" with no input or guidance from God, we will forfeit and **lose** God's better life for us with all His plans and purposes. The truth is, God knows what is best; I don't! He, after all, created each one of us, and He knows what is in us! By seeking God's Kingdom first and foremost, I enter God's blessings and plan for my life!

Abraham faced this challenge himself! Either to walk along the easier and more lucrative pathway-focused upon selfish ambition and this life's riches or to follow God's bidding! What is to be done in such circumstances when a challenge like this comes and stares you in the face, and you must make a choice?

Abraham's focus and priority, come what may, was always upon listening to and obeying God. In other words, he chose not to seek the way that seemed right to a man but to follow that which God showed him, which required faith and trust instigated by a heart that genuinely wanted God. **Denying yourself is** forsaking your own choices and, instead, seeking to fulfil God's purposes for His Kingdom. So Abraham gave up his selfish rights and chose to obey God unconditionally! Am I, and are you prepared to do that?

Abraham could well have thought that he had not come out of Ur of the Chaldees in response to God's call upon his life to be diverted by a fleshly appeasing obstacle seemingly. The rich plains by the Jordan river may have had all the appearances of attraction and desire for one to possess them, and they were there for the taking, but no, Abraham considered what God had promised him to be far more precious! Why leave everything in the first place if you are not prepared to follow it through? The plains of the Tigress and Euphrates rivers were also rich for that matter and not too far from his old home; they would have been just as fruitful and fertile as the plains of Jordan!

Consequently, Abraham did not regard the plains of Jordan as important as Lot, so, instead, he allowed his nephew to choose first. Clearly, God, seeing the heart and real desire of both Abraham and Lot, gave each one what they most desired; for the one, it was the pleasures of sin for a season - for that's what it turned out to be - but for the other, the freedom to walk before his God to fulfil His will.

A Testimony

A challenging circumstance that tested my faith early on in my life comes to mind at this point.

At the time, my wife and I had two young children and were living in lowly-rented accommodation in Acton, London. It essentially consisted of a mere two rooms joined by a small hallway. There came a season when I looked for a job promotion that would take us out of London, preferably to the countryside! Family often pressured us to move. They would say something like,

> "This is not the place to live and bring up children! Properties are far cheaper in the North of England."

Thus far, all applications for jobs had failed until one came along, for which I seemed to be perfectly qualified. I really believed this to be the one to go for!

After praying about it, I did not feel at peace! I thought of going for the interview, believing that I wouldn't get the job if it were not God's will, but I did not feel any peace about that scenario either! I became so burdened about everything.

After sharing all with my wife, we made our decision. I took the stamped, addressed job application letter and tore it into two pieces! Immediately after this dramatic turn of events, a surge of peace flooded into me like a river! You see, we were in God's will right there in those two rooms. God did not wish us to move at that time, and, in fact, He didn't take us away from London for a total of forty years!

When I retired at the age of sixty, we knew that our mission in London had been completed, so we moved to the countryside, which I love.

This scenario reminded me of when Lot separated his sheep from those of Abraham, choosing to dwell in the lush fields of Sodom, whereas Abraham went to live in the desert! I remembered this story about Abraham very well.

At the beginning of my walk with God, I began reading the Bible from Genesis, having first read one Gospel previously. It seemed the best place to start at the time, and Abraham's life of faith spoke to me and helped me in those early days, showing me how to walk by faith with God. I would rather be *in the wilderness* with God than doing my own thing, possibly ending up in "*Sodom*" just like Lot!

My wife and I had both prayed about the job scenario, asking God to show us the way forward, and that's what He did! We were attending a church nearby, where we received the Word of God and were engaged in ministry with children's work, teens leaders and open-air outreaches. Most of all, we were receiving good Bible study teaching, which has helped us for the rest of our lives. I had also been given opportunities to preach and become an elder!

There are times when God wants us to put the interests of His Kingdom above everything else so that He can build us up and equip us for what lies ahead, and this was undoubtedly one of them. If we commit our way to Him, He has promised to direct our path. We simply must trust Him with our lives.

At that time, God had already written upon my heart a Scripture that I heard preached on the day I came to The Lord.

> "Then Jesus said to His disciples, "If anyone desires to come after Me, let him deny himself, and take up his cross, and follow Me. For whoever desires to save his life will lose it, but whoever loses his life for My sake will find it. For what profit is it to a man if he gains the whole world, and loses his own soul? Or what will a man give in exchange for his soul?"
>
> **Matthew 16:24-26**

This passage, being already engraved upon my very soul, meant that I feared to do anything outside of God's will. Make no mistake; I wanted to go for the interview; I wanted to get a better job and leave London, preferring the country any day to city life, but not at the expense of losing God's blessing! I could not do it if The Lord were not with me! In our case, *the pillar of cloud* stood firm over our little flat in Acton, two rooms and all, and, simply, would not move!

It can be challenging to follow God, and my situation initially burdened me. There is always a tug between going God's way and going your own way! It is probably true to say that the tug is between the flesh and The Spirit! Yet, ultimately, there was no real obstacle! To follow God meant everything to me, so I gladly tore up the letter and felt very relieved in doing so. I trusted that God knew better, and by faith, both my wife and I carried on where we left off, with peace and full of joy, knowing that we were in God's will and He was right there with us!

When I asked my children years later where the happiest place they had lived was, guess their response? It was when we all lived a simple life in Acton in our little flat! You see, if children have a good loving relationship with their parents, they will prefer that to anything else and be content wherever they live. Anyway, if God allowed His Son to be born in a stable, what had I to complain about, living in two rooms?

There was a song we used to sing in our church hall in Acton. It went something like this:

"What matters where on Earth we dwell, on mountain top or in the dell, in cottage or in mansion fair, where JESUS is 'tis Heaven there!"

Where Jesus Is, Tis Heaven
James M. Black, 1898

We proved that obeying God and being in His will was all that mattered in life. He promised that if we sought His Kingdom first, all these other things would be added, and this we also proved!

After retiring and leaving London, having spent forty years in that city, we moved to Oxfordshire, joined a wonderful church, and carried on ministering.

Even as a born-again Christian, had I ignored The Holy Spirit's promptings and gone my own way, then I would have walked outside of God's will for my life! Learning obedience is an essential part of life as a child of God. I am saved at conversion, yes! But I am being continually saved throughout my life, being taught, tested, and tried! Then, ultimately, I shall be saved when Christ comes, or He takes me home!

Meditation

Were the whole realm of nature mine,
that were an offering far too small;
love so amazing, so divine,
demands my soul, my life, my all.
Isaac Watts, 1674-1748

"If anyone desires to come after Me, let him deny himself, and take up his cross, and follow Me."
Matthew16:24

Jesus never asks us to do anything He wouldn't do Himself.

DAY 15

Being Alone with God

"He who follows Me shall not walk in darkness but have the light of life."
John 8:12

When your walk with Christ becomes personal and real to you, when all distractions have been dealt with so that you feel free and unhindered, then you are not afraid to follow and obey Him wherever He leads!
Abraham had distractions all along the way since leaving Ur of the Chaldees. These were largely due to family members who were not of the same spiritual mind as him. Why should this be? Abraham, or rather, Abram as he was initially called, received the call of God and not another! God had said to him,

*"Get out of your country,**From your family And from your father's house,**To a land that I will show you. I will make you a great nation."*
Genesis 12: 1

The Bible says that Abraham stopped at Haran on his journey to Canaan, and some believe this could have been for several years until his father, Terah, had died. Most likely, it was very significant because Abraham's father, Terah, served other gods and worshiped idols. This fact is revealed later when Abraham's grandson, Jacob, served Laban to marry his daughter Rachael. (*Laban was the son of Bethuel, the son of Nahor, the son of Terah, Abraham's father.*)

> *"Now Laban had gone to shear his sheep, and* **Rachel had stolen the household idols that were her father's."**
>
> **Genesis 31:3**

These idolatrous connections in Abraham's camp would have been an obstruction to God's purposes and needed to be removed.

Likewise, a person today who follows The Lord will have serious problems if they come from a family that follows a different religion. In any case, those closest to you cannot understand the call of God upon your life, and Jesus mentioned that there could be hindrances in the form of well-intended advice that can distract you from following God and that these usually come from family members.

> *"He who loves father or mother more than Me is not worthy of Me. And he who loves son or daughter more than Me is not worthy of Me. And he who does not take his cross and follow after Me is not worthy of Me."*
>
> **Matthew 10: 37-38**

Jesus said this fully knowing the commandment, *"Honour your father and mother."*

Human feelings and lack of appreciation can easily confuse the issue. No parent would desire their son or daughter to go away somewhere that could be dangerous, even when doing what they believe to be God's plan and will for their lives. It is more difficult when family members do not know The Lord.

Furthermoremore, Abraham's nephew, Lot, accompanied him for much of the journey, which could have been arduous on occasions. Whilst it is normal for family members to argue and disagree at times, an occasion arose more serious than any disagreement when extreme strife erupted between Abraham and Lot over each other's herdsman and livestock!

> *"And there was strife between the herdsmen of Abram's livestock and the herdsmen of Lot's livestock…Abram said to Lot, "Please let there be no strife between you and me, and between my herdsmen and your herdsmen; for we are brethren."*
>
> **Genesis 13: 7-8**

We know what happened next; Lot went one way, east towards Sodom, and Abraham went west towards Canaan and, in doing so, continued walking in the will of God! Any outsider would have surely said,

"looks like Abraham drew the short straw!"

We always do well not to express adverse comments too quickly, or strongly interfere regarding the whereabouts of a person's dwelling or path in life they choose to take, especially when those concerned are God's children! I know this very well from personal experience! God's way is not our way, and sometimes He leads us in the most unlikely places that can be contrary to all human reasoning. Let us remember our Lord Himself was born in poverty, grew up with a simple family, and worked towards a carpentry trade, yet He was God manifest in the flesh! Is this not contrary to our expectations? He was sent and chosen by The Father to be The Saviour of the world! Jesus did not have a great education as far as this world is concerned, neither did He become rich in this world's goods which men would count as successful!

> *"For you know the grace of our Lord Jesus Christ, that though He was rich, yet for your sakes He became poor, that you through His poverty might become rich."*
> **2 Corinthians 8:9**

Now let us see what happens next, the moment Abraham departs from his nephew Lot.

> "And The Lord said to Abram, **after Lot had separated from him:** "Lift your eyes now and look from the place where you are – northward, southward, eastward, and westward; for all the land which you see I give to you and your descendants forever. And I will make your descendants as the dust of the earth; so that if a man could number the dust of the earth, then your descendants also could be numbered. Arise, walk in the land through its length and its width, for I give it to you."
>
> **Genesis 13: 14-17**

We notice straight away that God spoke personally to Abraham the moment he was separated from Lot! The time had arrived for God to deal differently and individually with Abraham, for it was now just him and God! All external distractions were gone with the absence of family connections. We shall see later that, whilst things were better now that the conflict with his nephew was over, Abraham experienced some personal difficulties.

Thus far, Abraham had passed the tests and remained faithful despite some distractions in Egypt along the way. God had been teaching him, and he submitted, a quality necessary for every child of God!

Such accounts of people like Abraham, who wholeheartedly followed God throughout their lifetime, are inspiring, and we can easily relate to them in their practical, real-life setting. It reminded me of an occasion when my wife and I met another such person whose life had been given to God to serve Him, and his testimony influenced us both.

It was a long time ago, in 1967. My then-fiancée and I attended a meeting, not that long after we, ourselves, came to The Lord, to listen to a missionary named William F.P. Burton. He was one of the first Pentecostal Pioneers in Central Africa in the early nineteen - hundreds and his mission field was then called The Congo. Over many years, he founded The Congo Evangelistic Mission that grew out of simple beginnings to more than 5,000 local churches.

When Mr. Burton spoke to us about his departure from England, flying from London to The Congo, he presented, to my mind, a humble picture that I will never forget. Mr. Burton had stood alone at the airport carrying a single suitcase holding his entire belongings! His life ahead would be spent totally serving God, pioneering unknown territory in Africa, and it wasn't going to be plain sailing. The following is an independent account of Mr. Burton's early experiences in The Congo.

> *"These were early days of fighting sickness, encountering cannibal tribesmen, learning the language and making the first maps of the country. As they went forth preaching, God confirmed his word with signs following and souls saved. Just after their initial arrival in 1915 the work commenced in the healing of a local native who was badly bent over and walking with sticks! Instantly he was healed and continued with a straight back for the next 33 years."*

"PENTECOSTAL PIONEERS REMEMBERED"
W.F.P. Burton (1886-1971)

His testimony impacted us both and sowed the desire to follow and serve The Lord wholeheartedly deep within our hearts. Not knowing the future and God's purposes and plans for our lives, we both went away thoughtful and changed! I believe this contributed to our outlook in life to serve God in whatever way He wanted.

Once a person has dedicated their whole life to serving God, they begin a closer journey with Him. They yield their decisions and choices to Him truly saying, *"not my will but yours be done,"* immediately having God's attention to a newer level! I have always believed this!

Meditation

I gave My life for thee,
My precious blood I shed,
That thou might ransomed be,
And raised up from the dead;
I gave, I gave My life for thee,
What hast thou giv'n for Me?
I gave, I gave My life for thee,
What hast thou giv'n for Me?

"I Gave My Life for Thee"
Frances R. Havergal, 1858

DAY 16

Jesus Christ is My Lord

One of the difficulties encountered by the children of Israel in the wilderness when God delivered them out of Egypt was not knowing the real purpose of their Salvation from God through lack of foresight and understanding. God desired then, and still does today, a personal relationship with man. He wants to be more than just a problem solver; He desires to be our Father! He created man in His own image for that reason, to have mutual fellowship. However, the children of Israel were selfishly thinking only about their own desires with a fleshly sense of lack since leaving Egypt. This perception of wanton lack dominated their insatiable lust for more and better provision! They forever compared their so-called plight in the wilderness to the wonderful garlic of Egypt! How often they would cry to Moses, loathing the manna and craving for meat!

> *"Now the mixed multitude who were among them yielded to intense craving; so, the children of Israel also wept again and said: "Who will give us meat to eat? We remember the fish which we ate freely in Egypt, the cucumbers, the melons, the leeks, the onions, and the garlic; but now our whole being is dried up; there is nothing at all except this manna before our eyes!"*
>
> **Numbers 11: 4-6**

God's Lordship over His people provided for unique, miraculous provision and power as He walked with them. Their shoes never wore out; they had food and water in the wilderness and were kept from sickness and disease! Yet they were continually dissatisfied, and their complaining brought upon them the judgement of God on more than one occasion.

In type, this may be compared to the lusts of the flesh, which war against The Spirit. Whilst God has given us a new nature born after His likeness, we can, by our longing and leaning towards the flesh, overrule by our choices, this new life God has given us and desire the old life of Egypt instead.

On Day 12, we looked at the *Flesh and The Spirit* reading the following Scriptures:

> *"There is therefore now no condemnation to those who are in Christ Jesus,* **who do not walk according to the flesh, but according to The Spirit."**
>
> **Romans 8: 1**

"For the flesh lusts against The Spirit, and The Spirit against the flesh; and these are contrary to one another, so that you do not do the things that you wish."
Galatians 5:17

Once man's unregenerate nature is regenerated (renewed or restored) by The Spirit of God, he becomes a Spiritual man. Yet, according to the above Scriptures, he must strive against the old nature, or rather, mortify its deeds, by continually putting them to death, for it is not subject to the law of God. We see, therefore, the necessity to walk in The Spirit. Yes, this entails walking according to God's Word, walking to please God, hence walking with God in a personal, cooperative, and obedient way that is more intimate. In doing so, He is not just my Saviour who has saved me from my sin but also, He is Lord of my life as He leads me on through *the wilderness,* teaching and correcting me each step of the way because He is a loving Father who cares for each one of His children! In other words, having been saved, we must choose to

follow on to know The Lord,

we can learn a lesson here from the Israelites who trekked in the wilderness for forty years! God knows what is best for our new spiritual lives with Him but are we willing to accept this and agree to walk with God? The Bible says,

"Can two walk together, unless they are agreed?"
Amos 3:3

Are we prepared to follow Him come what may – even if there may be no garlic or leeks!? Remember, the children of Israel were forty years wandering in the wilderness continually moaning because they would not walk with their God and accept Him as their Lord and Saviour. Consequently, except for Joshua and Caleb, only children born in the wilderness went into the promised land. The rest all died in the wilderness!

Is this not a tragedy that God was taking His people to the promised land, yet they never got there!? Instead, they wandered through life forty years! Does this not speak to us today? Think about all the promises that belong to us in Christ Jesus, yet we still fail to appreciate or embrace them in reality! As we shall see, the fulfilment of many of God's promises is conditional upon us receiving them! Because they are not necessarily commandments, we can choose not to pursue them! Search the Scriptures and see where God *invites His people* rather than commands them!

"If my people will...then I will hear"

> *"I beseech you therefore, brethren, by the mercies of God, ... that you may prove"*

> *"Try Me now in this... If I will not open for you the windows of heaven"*

I always find these promises challenging, but if I earnestly desire Jesus Christ to be my Lord, then love demands, I at least comply with God's desires for me to be blessed by Him whatever the sacrifice may be!

> *"Therefore, since a promise remains of entering His rest, let us fear lest any of you seem to have come short of it. For indeed The Gospel was preached to us as well as to them; but the word which they heard did not profit them, not being mixed with faith in those who heard it."*
>
> **Hebrews 4: 1-2**

Of course, in Christ, we are saved by His Grace alone through the Blood of Jesus, and He chastises us that we may walk according to The Spirit and not the flesh. Whilst He does this for our good because He loves us, even so, we can still wander far too long through life in a wilderness of our own choosing, following our own selfish choices and decisions that can never lead to true life. We are then like ten of the twelve spies sent to spy out the land before them, who gave a bad report because they were too afraid to go where God wanted them to go!

Jesus spoke some sobering words that still challenge believers to this very day!

> *"Not everyone who says to Me,* **'Lord, Lord,'** *shall enter the kingdom of heaven, but* **he who does the will of My Father in heaven.** *Many will say to Me in that day, 'Lord, Lord, have we not prophesied in Your name, cast out demons in Your name, and done many wonders in Your name?' And then I will declare to them,* **'I never knew you; depart from Me, you who practice lawlessness!'"**
>
> **Matthew 7: 21-23**

In this passage, Jesus says *I never knew you,* or I was *never aware of you!* Notice how Jesus emphasizes that His requirement of a **personal knowledge or relationship** with the persons concerned **was absent!** If there had been a personal relationship, Jesus would most certainly have known them. Upon one occasion, Jesus said to His followers:

> "**My sheep** hear My voice, and **I know them**, and they follow Me."
>
> **John 10:27**

Jesus effectively motivated His disciples to ensure they lived authentically and truthfully by obeying Him and doing The Father's will. Such righteous living comes from the heart with love and trust, not through a law's observance, an external code of conduct, or ethics. Here Jesus is revealing the difference between a *correct behaviour* based upon the Law and *righteous actions* that proceed from the heart of a new, born-again life in Christ. We must never undervalue the importance of obeying God out of a pure heart! Unlike observance to laws, God sees and beholds the motive for all we do!

Who we are is seen and known only by the fruit of The Spirit displayed in our life. Such fruit is far more important to God than all the things I profess to have done for His Kingdom! Remember, Jesus said *by their fruits you shall know them!* If the world's standards are *quantity*, then God's standards are *quality* so let us never judge ourselves or any apparent success by the world's standards. Worldly popularity and approval are no sure sign of having God's approval!

Prayer

- *Lord Jesus, I ask You this day to be both my Lord and Saviour.*
- *I come to You in prayer now to ask You to help me follow Your way for my life.*
- *Teach me Your Word.*
- *Help me, for I do not always know the reality of Your presence.*
- *I yield myself to You now and believe You will receive me through Your Son Jesus Christ.*

Amen.

DAY 17

The Fountain of Living Water

> *"Ho! Everyone who thirsts,*
> *Come to the waters,*
> *And you who have no money,*
> *Come, buy, and eat."*
>
> **Isaiah 55:1**

God's invitations to all mankind to come to Him are by no means few! The two Scriptures below contain such a request, and there are many more!

> *"...the one who **comes to Me** I will by no means cast out."*

> ***"Come to Me**, all you who labour and are heavy laden, and I will give you rest."*

Essentially, God is inviting us to have an abundant life in Him. The real question is this,

Am I thirsty for more of God?

When you have been walking on a journey for a good while, especially when it is a hot day, there comes a time when you are thirsty and need a drink. Eventually, as time passes, your mind becomes set upon it so much that you cannot think of anything else! The money in your pocket cannot help if shops are far afield. Similarly, when walking with God *on the road* for a while, you can acquire an insatiable appetite with a deep desire and longing for something more, having tasted and seen that The Lord is good! The Bible presents such a picture of one of God's creations in such a state.

> *"As the deer pants for the water brooks,*
> *So pants my soul for You, O God.*
> *My soul thirsts for God, for the living God."*
> **Psalms 42:1-2**

The deer will smell water a long distance away and speeds in haste in that direction with an intense desire and longing to satisfy its thirst! Furthermore, a stream or river is a place of safety from the enemy! Why is this? Well, there are other forms of God's creation, and just as the deer can smell the water, so they can smell the deer! Predators will seek and follow the smell of deer with a similar longing for food as the deer has for water! When the deer reaches a river, it can wade through the water, hide its tracks, and throw off any hunters and killers. Our bodies need water! Our souls need the Living water!

One day, not long after I had been born again and filled with The Holy Spirit, I was sat in a student's prayer meeting at University with three or four other students. There seemed a deadness in the meeting. Sometimes it is good to be quiet - but this? It was so quiet it was tangible, and you could cut the atmosphere with a knife!

Suddenly, the unction of The Spirit came upon me. I knew in my heart what was needed; we were all thirsty; we required a refreshing and some invigoration; we needed some Living Water! Quite boldly, I *spoke in Tongues,* followed by an interpretation that went something like this,

> *"If you come to God with a cup, He will fill it;*
> *If you come to God with a bucket, He will fill it.*
> *If you come to God with a very large empty vessel,*
> *He will fill that too!*
> *I will fill your vessel according to what you bring to Me."*

After the meeting had ended, a young man said to me, *"Why is it that whenever you pray, I feel the presence of God? When you were praying and speaking, I felt a liberating sensation of power and God's presence."*

"It is The Holy Spirit," I said!

He had received something from God and now looked glowing, having his countenance somewhat more flushed and his eyes shining radiantly! I will never forget that occasion, and it served as a pointer to me for the rest of my life that this is what God does! He moves in the realm of His Holy Spirit to bring down help and blessing! But the question both then and now is the same.

"Am I thirsty for more of God? Do I desire His Presence and abundance of life for myself? Do I long for the reality of God speaking to me? Am I prepared to seek Him and seek Him more until I get to the brook for Living Water? Will I pant after Him like the deer; seek Him, call upon Him until He quenches my thirst and my longing desire for more of Him?"

Let this be a word from The Lord to you personally, today, for His river never runs dry!

"I will fill your vessel according to what you give to Me."

"Blessed are those who hunger and thirst for righteousness, for they shall be filled."
Matthew 5:6

It is abundantly clear to me that the fullness and overflowing of The Spirit of God are so essential to living a victorious life. Our human self can be such a hindrance to the moving of God's Spirit, as the above example demonstrates, and that is why God's Holy Spirit is at hand to impart His words of encouragement. God can move despite us, but the reality is this, He can bring life into a gathering and set us free! The flesh and human effort will never be able to draw upon God's presence, but The Spirit working through us can! *That which is flesh is flesh, and that which is Spirit is Spirit!* May God make each one of us like a fountain of life, issuing words of wisdom and encouragement, according to God's Word, by The Spirit when required!

This fullness and overflowing are not from human efforts seeking to express joyful enthusiasm! Rather, it is a moving of The Spirit exhibiting joy unspeakable and full of glory! That which is of The Spirit of God will always be experienced as a blessing to those around. Its effect will be positive and edifying. The Spirit of God is not the author of confusion. A truly Spirit-filled life is abundant life and is always expressed and exhibited in the form of love for God and His Word and love for others. Therefore, let us continually seek to be filled with The Holy Spirit, bringing before God a thirsty empty vessel for Him to fill so that it may then poured out upon others as a blessing, edification, and release!

"For God has not given us a spirit of fear, but of **power and of love and of a sound mind.**"

2 Timothy 1: 7

The Holy Spirit is the conveyor that transports the love of God into the human soul bringing freedom and release

At the end of the feast of tabernacles, before The Holy Spirit came on the Day of Pentecost, Jesus proclaimed to a multitude calling all that were thirsty to believe in Him and out of their inner-most being would flow rivers of Living Water!

> *"On the last day, that great day of the feast, Jesus stood and cried out, saying,* **"If anyone thirsts, let him come to Me and drink. He who believes in Me, as the Scripture has said, out of his heart will flow rivers of living water."** *But this He spoke concerning* **The Spirit**, *whom those believing in Him would receive; for The Holy Spirit was not yet given, because Jesus was not yet glorified."*

John 7: 37-39

The purpose of these outward manifestations of The Spirit of God, in every generation, is to use them, as The Spirit leads, to edify and strengthen one another in Christ. Members of the body, when assembled, can seek to be used by God to bless others through the gifts or enabling of The Spirit. These gifts were encouraged for edification in the early church, providing that all things were done decently and in order!

> *"How is it then, brethren? Whenever you come together, each of you has a psalm, has teaching, has a tongue, has a revelation, has an interpretation. Let all things be done for edification."*
> **1 Corinthians 14:26**

In Old Testament times, the eyes of the people were blind. They learned about God in the Law regarding His requirements on how they should live and approach Him, and yet, the eyes of their heart were blind because the way into His presence was not yet open to them, and a veil separated them.

> *"But even to this day, when Moses is read,* **a veil lies on their heart.** *Nevertheless, when one turns to The Lord,* **the veil is taken away.** *Now The Lord is The Spirit; and* **where The Spirit of The Lord is, there is liberty."** *(freedom)*
> **2 Corinthians 3: 15-17**

For every born-again believer, there is a place of liberty and freedom for them to enter through The Spirit of God! Through faith in Christ and the power of The Spirit, the veil is removed from the eyes of our hearts, and God reveals His glory to us in the person of Jesus Christ. He is not a respecter of persons! Therefore, all who come to Christ have the door of The Spirit realm opened to them, whereby they can walk together with The Spirit of God, rejoicing in The Lord Jesus and obeying God's Word.

"Remember, to be born- again is to be born of The Spirit of God." (Days 3 and 5)

Sin is what holds the veil in place, and forgiveness of sin is what removes the veil. In coming to Jesus, we receive forgiveness of sins and are therefore made free from the bondage of sin. The actions of The Spirit of God bringing liberty and freedom are real, experiential expressions or outward manifestations confirming to each believer that these things are so! God does not want us merely to have a theoretical understanding of His Word but to know that His Word is the Living Word! God desires us to receive His Salvation and rejoice in it with all our heart, mind and soul! Only by The Spirit can we see and know that we have been saved, forgiven and now belong to God through Jesus! The Spirit always confirms and bears witness to the Word of God! This news is so incredible that we need The Holy Spirit to help us give it justice! As the Scripture proclaims,

> *"Though now you do not see Him, yet believing,* ***you rejoice with joy inexpressible and full of glory!"***
>
> **1 Peter 1:8**

The Spirit and The Word are always fused to give life and not death, to impart life and not just knowledge, facts, and information! As it is written,

> *"God, who also made us (Paul and the apostles) sufficient as ministers of the new covenant,* ***not of the letter but of The Spirit; for the letter kills, but The Spirit gives life."***
>
> **2 Corinthians 3: 6**

As we close this session, lets us be inspired to seek after God as we have never done before! If we have seen and realised anything at all today, it is this:

- *God requires me to be thirsty for more of Him.*
- *Being born-again of The Spirit means just that! God's Spiritual realm is open for me to enter.*
- *The Holy Spirit is to play a vital role in my walk with God.*

Day 18

Desire the Pure Milk of the Word

Quenching our thirst with water is a specific, howbeit, extremely essential, and important requirement! The adult human body is comprised of about 60% of water and would not live for very long without it. That being said, our bodies cannot live for that long without food and sustenance either though some have tried it only to fail. That's how we are made, and indeed most other creatures are the same; we need food and water!

The amount and type of food we eat are progressive. A baby can only digest milk and very soft liquid food; then, gradually, solids become the order of the day! When the teeth come through, it won't be long before they eat meat!

A staple diet for most of us is bread, but in other countries around the world, it may be rice or another carbohydrate food, the body's primary source of energy that the body turns into glucose.

So, it is spiritually. We begin as babes in Christ, requiring milk to grow.

> *"Therefore, laying aside all malice, all deceit, hypocrisy, envy, and all evil speaking, **as newborn babes, desire the pure milk of the word, that you may grow thereby...**"*
> **1 Peter 2:1-2**

Notice how it is a pre-requisite to put aside several negative things of the old life before proceeding with the Word of God. We are told to lay aside *all malice, all deceit, hypocrisy, envy, and all evil speaking*

God always desires to show us the way we should go, and He expects us to adhere and be compliant to His instructions. We **learn to walk with God** as we submit to His way. Our attentiveness to His voice will lead us into abundant life!

Spiritual growth is like natural growth, and this parallel is used in the Bible, where it compares the pure milk of The Word with growth in God. In this verse, we are encouraged to,

"... ***desire*** *the pure milk of the Word.* "

It is an eternal Word that will never pass away; it is reliable and trustworthy, yet we must desire it! We must learn to devout ourselves to keep and honour it. Remember that God's relationship with us is based upon love and obedience and entails free will and freedom of choice.

When He created mankind, you see, God did not wish for robots that would automatically do as He commanded, but He desired a relationship based upon choice. He wants me to choose to obey Him because I love Him, revere Him and acknowledge that He is right in every situation! Jesus says that *if you love Me, then you will keep My commandments*. Realise that if you love someone, it entails unreserved committment, trust, faithfulness, and God requires no less!

God's Word teaches us that our Creator has a unique and perfect plan for each one of His children.

> *"For I know the thoughts that I think toward you, says The Lord, thoughts of peace and not of evil, to give you a future and a hope."*
> **Jeremiah 29:11**

Furthermore, God's plan is perfect because He has imparted within each of His children specific giftings to enable them to perform good works! Before we were born, God saw each one of us from Eternity, and He chose what we could achieve for His Glory and Kingdom uniquely! That makes us special!

> **"For we are His workmanship, created in Christ Jesus for good works, which God prepared beforehand that we should walk in them."**
> **Ephesians 2:10**

Therefore, do not be surprised if your experiences are different from others! You and you alone can do the good works ordained by God for you, and no one else can! Just as each person is a unique creation, so also are the good works God has chosen for you to do. No one else can stand in your space; you are indispensable! Each person is essential to the overall fulfilment of God's purposes!

I cannot emphasize enough, the key to moving forward along God's pathway for your life is that you unreservedly believe that God's way is right and trustworthy. Therefore, *commit your way to The Lord, and He will direct your path.* Believe in Him; place your life in His hands and follow Him forever!

Remember, faith in God works by love. That is, we need to yield ourselves to His will in all things. We need to be extra diligent not to disregard opportunities of doing God's will by simply failing to do them! If we ever feel convicted in our conscience that God desires us to walk in a particular direction, instead of another, for example, going to the Bible Study or Prayer Meeting, and not elsewhere, then be sure that The Holy Spirit is seeking to direct your path. He may have something specific for you to hear at a particular meeting, so obey His call upon your life!

I remember studying the words *repent* and *repentance* on one occasion, and that week when Thursday evening came around, I firmly believe God wanted me to attend the Young People's meeting in the church. It was not normally meant for me as I had a Bible Study on a different evening, but I went along anyway and sat at the back of the room. The subject being taught was *Repent and Repentance,* and I learned all I needed to know right up to this very day!

God will always be faithful to us; we must learn to be faithful to Him. God continually makes allowances for us and forgives us. He *will never leave us or forsake us*! Remember that He loves us with an everlasting love! So, if we should stumble, as all will at some time, we will just get up and carry on, seeking this time to do the right thing! Through this process of following and being obedient to The Spirit against our own will, we learn to walk with God. It is opposite to our old human nature, whereby we would automatically pursue our own will and desires. Learn this! Follow Jesus always! It is better to please God than to seek favour or acceptance from man!

There is always going to be a conflict between the flesh and The Spirit! To progress with God, we must learn what it means to *walk in The Spirit, not to fulfill the lusts of the flesh.*

> "...For those who live according to the flesh set their minds on the things of the flesh, **but those who live according to The Spirit, the things of The Spirit.**"
>
> **Romans 8:5**

As We learn not to disobey The Spirit of God within us, even in what we may perceive to be *small matters,* we will be growing up in The Lord!

God called Abraham *His friend* because He knew him, and David *a man after His own heart*! Therefore, he has no favourites; Our seeking Him first and obeying His word is what God desires.

At the very beginning, I did not realise that God was calling me to go to His House regularly with far more commitment than I was demonstrating in my life! I had not recognised how vital this was for my growth and spiritual well-being. The Holy Spirit began to weigh heavy upon me until I realised that it was God inside of me calling me to come to Him and go to church!

There was a communion service, for example, that I had never known about though my church called it *The Breaking of Bread* service. The moment I responded, I felt at peace and experienced liberty once again. You see, I always prayed to do God's will, and therefore God responded and required me to do just that! God held me at my word! I had given my will over to Him, and in love, He called me into obedience. In this way, I was submitting to His will and not my own. The fact was that when I attended my first *Breaking of Bread Service*, I was so very moved by it! It was very personal to hear people thanking Jesus for dying for their sins and being forgiven! I heard gifts of The Spirit in operation, which edified the church *bringing down* God's presence! It was just as if God was speaking to me right there and then. Such experiences began to have a much deeper hold over me. I was captivated and awestruck by the presence and reality of God when attending a meeting!

My heart began to change dramatically towards God. I wanted to know Him more! I wanted Him in my life to the full! So, consequently, I attended every possible meeting that I could to obtain more of the Word of God and receive all the fellowship I could get with His people!

Finally, I believe very much, and even more so as the time of The Lord's Second Coming grows nearer, that we do well to never depart from the simplicity of The Gospel of Jesus Christ and the truth and infallibility of the Word of God. Time brings along with it many changes to our world, its attitudes and behaviour. The age is already upon us where some from *within the church* say,

"We need to move into the 21st century and change our ways and beliefs!"

Beware! This ploy is a plot from the enemy! In the last days[3] , many people will find the Bible and its teaching inconvenient and incompatible with their sinful lifestyle. Ironically, but not surprisingly, this is increasingly coming from religious people in high places who compromise long-standing beliefs in God and the Bible to accommodate modern, secular views! To retain their respectability, position, and power, they will surrender to blasphemous doctrines and ideologies!

Remember the Word of God says,

*"Heaven and earth will pass away, but **My words will by no means pass away**."*
Matthew 24:35

Prayer

---

[3] Living Victoriously in The last Days

Lord Jesus, thank You for Your unchanging love.

Thank You that I can learn to walk with You - something I could never have dreamed was possible. Help me by Your Holy Spirit walk in Your will for my life, and do those good works You prepared for me to do.

I realise that this world is passing away so please help me focus upon You above all other things. I wish to be where You are, above all this world's riches, wealth, and fame.

*Fill me with **Your** Holy Spirit; **Your** power to witness and **Your** Love to win people for **Your** Kingdom.*

<div align="right">Amen</div>

Day 19

The Bread of Life

As a child, I had a reputation for always being hungry! Unlike today, when Dad sometimes prepares the meal, and children tend to eat whenever they are hungry, in those days you had to eat the meals prepared by Mum, and only at mealtimes! If you were still hungry after your meal, you were told, *"get some bread and jam or bread and dripping!"*

And if you didn't want any of that, what would follow was, *"Get yourself some toast then!"*

Making toast was quite good, but it depended on whether the open coal fire had burned down enough to have plenty of red-hot coals. If so, we simply stabbed the bread with a long brass fork and toasted it over the hot coals, and within seconds it was done! You see, there were no electric toasters in our house! However, the taste of the toast was far superior when done over the fire and slathered with plenty of butter - it was delicious. One time, I remember eating six slices of toast! Well, they were only thin slices! When I eventually tried toast done in an electric toaster, I didn't like it that much! It was just not the same!

How hungry are we for the things of The Spirit and the Word of God? As we see, spiritual matters were revealed and manifested by Jesus but not without controversy. Initially, Jesus was criticised for performing miracles whenever He healed on the Sabbath day. Later, when He began to focus on who He was and that He alone could give mankind eternal life, the people reacted with unbelief, for they failed to see Him as anything other than a mere man, a prophet, and no more.

For example, Jesus identified Himself as *the Living Bread that came down from Heaven*. This concept was spiritual. It was new and difficult to understand, even by His disciples.

> *"And Jesus said to them, '**I am the bread of life**. He who comes to Me shall never hunger, and he who believes in Me shall never thirst.'"*
>
> **John 6:35**

> *"I am the living bread which came down from heaven. If anyone eats of this bread, he will live forever; and the bread that I shall give is My flesh, which I shall give for the life of the world."*
> *...The Jews therefore quarrelled among themselves, saying, '**How can this Man give us His flesh to eat?**'"*
>
> **John 6: 51-52**

Jesus had performed many miracles and signs before the people, but now He goes far deeper with His teaching. He makes it personal, focusing on Himself as the source and the giver of Eternal life, which was much more challenging! The eyes of all in the crowd pointed in one direction – towards Him! It was needful for them to see and recognise Jesus for who He really was because eternal life depended upon it! Until now, they only saw Him as Joseph, the carpenter's son.

The fact was that Jesus, who stood speaking to the people, was none other than God incarnate, the Eternal Son of the Living God! Oh! That their eyes could have beheld Him for who He was and still is! But for this illumination, they needed the help of The Holy Spirit who alone reveals Christ, and for this to happen, they needed to receive and believe upon Him as it is written,

> *"But without faith it is impossible to please Him, for he who comes to God must **believe that He is**, and that He is a rewarder of those who diligently seek Him."*
>
> **Hebrews 11:6**

And so, it is the same situation today. Nothing has changed. We must tell people that they need to come to Jesus believing in Him, for He alone has the power in Heaven and upon earth to grant eternal life.

> ***"He who believes in the Son has everlasting life**; and he who does not believe the Son shall not see life, but the wrath of God abides on him."*
>
> **John 3:36**

The background to this situation is worth considering. Firstly, the people were poor! Their life consisted of continual toil and hard work endeavouring to make provision for themselves and their families. It was no different for the parents and family of Jesus.

> *"For you know the grace of our Lord Jesus Christ, that **though He was rich, yet** **for your sakes He became poor, that** **you through His poverty might become** **rich."***

2 Corinthians 8: 9

Furthermore, they lived under oppression from a foreign power; they lived in bondage; they were not free! Many therefore looked upon the coming promised Messiah as the one who would deliver them from Roman rule and occupation. This was not to be!

Have you ever been in a situation when times were very hard! If so, how did you react if the situation you found yourself in was so difficult that you could hardly focus upon anything else? In such cases, it is more challenging to do the right thing and focus upon Christ than upon those contrary circumstances that can so easily consume you!

Today, we see unprecedented troubles in the world, such as floods, famines, earthquakes, world pandemics and pestilences! However, Jesus has promised never to leave us or forsake us, so always remember that He will never abandon His people or cast them off during these difficult times! On the contrary, He told us that such things would happen in the last days, did He not? Jesus said,

> *"And you will hear of wars and rumours of wars. See that you are not troubled; for all these things must come to pass, but the end is not yet. For nation will rise against nation, and kingdom against kingdom. And **there will be famines, pestilences, and earthquakes** in various places."*
> **Matthew 24: 6-7**

> *"These things I have spoken to you, that in Me you may have peace. In the world you will have tribulation; but be of good cheer, I have overcome the world."*
> **John 16: 33**

Remember, during such times of tribulation, God tests His people, searching their hearts to see where their focus and trust lie! In such circumstances, life is tough, but we still have victory through our Lord Jesus Christ! These troubles and world catastrophes highlight the need for us all to re-assess our priorities and our real purpose and role in this life. The sober fact is, our lives are temporary upon this earth, transitory and passing away like a fading flower. Although we already know this, we are surprised when suddenly, the world is spinning out of control and is in chaos. Only by focusing upon Christ can we remain at peace in readiness for His second coming. God promises,

> *"Because you have made The Lord, who is my refuge, Even the Most High your dwelling place, **no evil shall befall you, nor shall any plague come near your dwelling.**"*
> **Psalm 91: 9-10**

Therefore, it was tough for Jesus to stand and proclaim Himself as *the Bread of Life* and the source of eternal life when the people were diverted by poverty and oppression. "*What about the here and now?*" the crowd might say!
Jesus continued,

> *"Most assuredly, I say to you, you seek Me, not because you saw the signs, but because you ate of the loaves and were filled.* **Do not labour for the food which perishes, but for the food which endures to everlasting life, which the Son of Man will give you,"**
>
> John 6: 26-27

The people changed the subject,

> *"What shall we do, that we may work the works of God?"*
>
> John 6:28

Jesus answered knowing full well of their unbelief towards Him and said to them,

> *"This is the work of God, that you believe in Him whom He sent."*
>
> **John 6:29**

Sadly, this can be the state of modern-day believers who can be more interested in their role and doing those works that appeal to them most. Jesus would have none of it! He refused to be caught up in their thinking and instead pointed them to what was more needful – to believe upon Him!

Regarding our works for God, we can get it so wrong! It is not a matter of me working for God doing those things that I choose to do. It is not about me! It is God who chooses to live His life within us, performing His works through us! He gives us giftings to perform those good works ordained for us from the foundation of the world.

> *"For we are His workmanship,* **created in Christ Jesus for good works, which God prepared beforehand that we should walk in them."**
> **Ephesians 2: 10**

Jesus goes to the very heart of all that man thinks regarding his perceived purpose and role by telling them to believe in Him. The outstanding issue was that the crowd were simply not believing in Jesus! Their eyes were still upon the loaves and fishes! What they had received was more important than He who gave it! They were interested in this kind of miracle, namely that which would provide for the here and now! Yes, our physical lives are important to God, but this was not the whole story. This life is transitory, and Jesus told the people of their real need to believe in Him to have eternal life! There is a *food* that endures to eternal life, a Divine life that will continue forever, and this *food* is found in Christ alone! Therefore, we should ask ourselves the following questions:

- *What am I hungry and thirsty for?*
- *Are we just like the crowd?*
- *Is my focus purely upon what Jesus can do for me to the omission of all else?*

If our attention is entirely upon the *here and now*, we will miss the real reason why Jesus came, and that was to give us eternal life! Like the crowd, we can solely focus upon transient things belonging to this life only and forget the real goal of eternal life through faith in Christ. Jesus went even furthermore and did not restrain His words to appease them,

> *"He who eats My flesh and drinks My blood abides in Me, and I in him. As the living Father sent Me, and I live because of The Father, so he who feeds on Me will live because of Me."*
> **John 6:56-57**

The Jews failed to understand that Jesus was speaking Spiritually, which was another of their problems. Like so many today, they could see no furthermore than themselves and their circumstances. Their perceived needs were obvious to them, and they only related to the present day! By believing in Jesus, a person can obtain spiritual eyesight and understand that far greater things are at stake, not temporal or short-lived but eternal! By rejecting Jesus, they remained lost and blind to anything God would have shown them.

The battle is this! When problems divert us and focus upon them, we can become, just like the crowd, so consumed by our distress and difficulties turning our eyes away from The Lord! This was their problem in part, and if we are not careful, it can be ours too!

> *"Therefore, let him who thinks he stands take heed lest he fall."*
> **1 Corinthians 10:12**

Later, Jesus clarified things to His disciples and said,

> ***"It is The Spirit who gives life; the flesh profits nothing. The words that I speak to you are spirit, and they are life."***
> **John 6: 63**

The giving of Christ's flesh and the shedding of His blood upon the cross has provided the sinner a cleansing fountain of life to be washed free of their sins and receive eternal life. By coming to Christ and believing in Him, a person enters this flow, providing his inner man life and nourishment. To receive eternal life is to receive Him and Him only.

Another stumbling block to the world today is that people would rather seek to do their own good works and follow a belief system that appeases their desires than to humble themselves before Christ; such is the pride and arrogance of sinful man!

The Jews had a different problem to that of their lack of perception and understanding of spiritual matters. There is a certain issue that Jesus Himself referred to, and a prophet is not without honour except in his own country. As mentioned, Jesus was the son of Joseph - and that was it!

> *"And many.... were astonished, saying,*
> *"Where did this Man get these things? And what wisdom is this which is given to Him, that such mighty works are performed by His hands! Is this not the carpenter, the Son of Mary, and brother of James, Joses, Judas, and Simon? And are not His sisters here with us?" So, they were offended at Him."*
> **Mark 6: 2-3**

Although the crowds were astonished by the many miracles Jesus performed, their rejection was aggravated by pride. The difficulty here was accepting that the carpenter, Jesus the son of Joseph, could declare Himself to be **the Bread of Life** and that eternal life was to be found in Him! Therefore, do not be surprised if people reject your words out of pride and contempt, however true they may be!

Finally, we will look at a completely different scenario, one that comes to mind in stark contrast to the opinions and attitudes of the crowd that we have just seen. One day, Jesus healed a man born blind on the Sabbath! The man in question did not know who Jesus was though undoubtedly, he would have heard about Him. The Pharisees confronted him soon after and told him to denounce Jesus for healing upon the Sabbath, stipulating that Jesus could not have come from God because he had done such a thing! The man spoke boldly and bravely to them in response,

"Why, this is a marvellous thing, that you do not know where He is from; yet He has opened my eyes! Now we know that God does not hear sinners; but if anyone is a worshiper of God and does His will,
He hears him. Since the world began it has been unheard of that anyone opened the eyes of one who was born blind. ***If this Man were not from God, He could do nothing."***

John 9: 30-33

"Jesus heard later that they had cast him out; and when He had found him, He said to him,
   "Do you believe in the Son of God?"
He answered and said,
   "Who is He, Lord, that I may believe in Him?"
And Jesus said to him,
   "You have both seen Him and it is He who is talking with you."

Then he said,
> *"Lord, I believe!" And he worshiped Him.*

And Jesus said,
> *"For judgment I have come into this world, that those who do not see may see, and that those who see may be made blind.""*
> **John 9: 35-39**

Why was this attitude shown by the blind man not reciprocated by the crowd who also witnessed an amazing miracle that benefited them all?! The reaction here, displayed by the man born blind, is a most wonderful picture and example of humble gratitude and faith shown towards Jesus. The poor blind man, having been healed, stood up to the Pharisees defending Jesus. Nowhere else do I read of someone doing this! It is exceptional, and one must wonder how Jesus felt about this wonderful testimony coming from such an unlikely source. So much so that the Bible says Jesus went after him.

> *"And when **He had found him**, He said to him **"Do you believe in the Son of God?"***
> **John 9:35**

What a blessing it is to see this kind of faith and submission! How gracious and kind is The Lord to those who believe in Him with a compliant and submissive heart, those who will trust Him utterly and completely!

Prayer

Dear Lord, I come to focus upon You above all else.
    Help me when I am tempted to be diverted towards other things when it's You, Oh Lord, that I need most of all in my life.
Lead me by Your Holy Spirit that I might be joyful in You and Your salvation.
    Save me O Lord when distress would overcome me and lead me to the rock that is higher than I!

Meditation

Like those in the crowd, am I more concerned about what work I might do for God rather than seeking to establish a deeper personal relationship with Jesus and making Him my focus and priority in life?

Am I also like those in the crowd seeking for God to perform those miracles that appease my comfort in this life, only forgetting that my priorities must first and foremost be upon what matters for Eternity?

PART 4

The Holy Spirit

Day 20

A Prophecy

The last days began when Jesus came to this earth and they will last until He comes again.

> *"God, who at various times and in various ways spoke in time past to The Fathers by the prophets, has, in these last days, spoken to us by His Son…"*
> **Hebrews:1: 1-2**

"There is a sense of finality about the words "last days" mentioned here right at the beginning of the book of Hebrews. The writer in this statement refers to God's involvement in history – from days long ago when He spoke to individuals, to a people, to a nation by the prophets – but now God has spoken to the world through His Son, Jesus Christ. No longer does God speak just to a privileged nation, Israel; now, everyone is included – you and me, too."
Quote: "Living Victoriously in The Last Days"

Brian Reddish

The "last days" are already over two thousand years old, yet they are described as "last!" However, the point to realise here is not so much the duration of time spanning the period called "the last days" but the dispensation and period in God's programme that they represent. In coming to this earth, Jesus has ushered in a new era – the days of God's Grace towards all mankind! Time, however, has an end! It is well on its way to running its course towards completion. As it is written,

> " ...the end of all things is at hand..."
>
> **1 Peter 4: 7a**

It is well said that *time waits for no man!* Time has a destination like a river that runs a course until it runs into the estuary at the sea, and will one day come to an end. At the sea, the river ceases; so, it will be when God's programme comes to an end; time will cease!
Jesus lived no more than about thirty-three years upon this earth as a man. How little time was that compared with the overall duration of the last days thus far! Yet, whilst on earth, Jesus announced to His disciples something very special that would continue His Person and presence with them forever!

> *"But now I go away to Him who sent Me...*
> *...Nevertheless, I tell you the truth. It is to your advantage that I go away; for if I do not go away, the Helper will not come to you; but if I depart, I will send Him to you..."*
>
> **John 16: 5-7**

The coming of The Holy Spirit was what Jesus was referring to, and He, being God, would come and abide with them so that they could still know the presence of Jesus and be comforted by Him. Jesus was gracious, showing lovingkindness to His disciples, for they had lived with him for several years and would surely miss Him - but not for long! An amazing event
was to take place as prophesied a long time before, and it was this - the Coming of The Holy Spirit which would herald the birth of the Church! After Jesus rose, He told His disciples to wait in Jerusalem.

> *"Behold, I send the Promise of My Father upon you; but tarry in the city of Jerusalem until you are endued with power from on high."*
>
> **Luke 24: 49**

It was, of course, on the Day of Pentecost that The Holy Spirit came and in a dramatic fashion!

> *"When the Day of Pentecost had fully come, they were all with one accord in one place. And suddenly there came a sound from heaven, as of a rushing mighty wind, and it filled the whole house where they were sitting. Then there appeared to them divided tongues, as of fire, and one sat upon each of them and they were all filled with The Holy Spirit and began to speak with other tongues, as The Spirit gave them utterance."*
>
> **Acts 2: 1-4**

Peter stood up before a very great crowd to explain what was happening!

> "...Peter, standing up with the eleven, raised his voice and said to them, "Men of Judea and all who dwell in Jerusalem, let this be known to you, and heed my words. For these are not drunk, as you suppose since it is only the third hour of the day. But this is what was spoken by the prophet Joel."
> **Acts 2: 14-16**

By The Holy Spirit, Peter spoke of a prophecy from the Old Testament book of Joel, which previously must have seemed puzzling to many a reader!

> "And it shall come to pass in the last days, says God,That I will pour out of My Spirit on all flesh;Your sons and your daughters shall prophesy,Your young men shall see visions,Your old men shall dream dreams and, on My menservants, and on My maidservants I will pour out My Spirit in those days; And they shall prophesy.I will show wonders in heaven above And signs in the earth beneath: Blood and fire and vapor of smoke. The sun shall be turned into darkness,And the moon into blood, Before the coming of the great and awesome day of The Lord.And it shall come to pass That whoever calls on the name of The Lord Shall be saved."
> **Acts 2: 17-21**
> **(Joel 2: 28-32)**

After our Lord's ascension into Heaven, the above phenomenon ear-marked the age of the Church, His Body, upon the earth, and was probably the second most important event to take place in the last days.

The first and most significant event in history was God speaking to us through His Son in lowly Galilee and, after that, God speaks, by the power of The Holy Spirit, through His Church, the Body of Christ, to the world! It is God's power and presence within ordinary men and women that have separated the last days from any other period in history! God has committed His born-again children to represent Him and His Word as ambassadors on the earth, reconciling man to God.

> *"Now then, we are ambassadors for Christ, as though God were pleading through us: we implore you on Christ's behalf, be reconciled to God."*
> **2 Corinthians 5: 20**

In the Old Testament, the power of The Holy Spirit was largely limited to The Spiritual and national leaders of Israel, but, under the New Covenant, the power and authority of The Holy Spirit are for *"all flesh"*. To *"pour out of My Spirit"* implies great abundance, not just a trickle! We may ask, What is God doing? He is fulfilling the promise Jesus made to His disciples when He said,

> *"I will come to you"* and on another occasion,

> *"... you shall receive power when The Holy Spirit has come upon you; and you shall be witnesses to Me in Jerusalem, and in all Judea and Samaria, and to the end of the earth*

Acts 1:8

God was equipping His disciples with His power to take His Word to the uttermost parts of the earth! Furthermore, *"All flesh"* is significant and means God pours out His Spirit, not upon every individual, but those who believe in Him of all classes and nations of people, whether young or old, men or women - all who believe irrespective of their status! What is even more unprecedented is that God promised to pour out His Spirit upon *"My menservants and on My maidservants!"* In the Old Testament, this was not the privilege of such people! There does not seem to be any example where a slave functioned as a prophet!? Perhaps most importantly, Peter does not see the Coming of The Spirit as relegated and confined to the Apostles and those believers of that day since he stipulates that it is for every generation – as many as The Lord our God shall call!

> *"...For the promise is to you and to your children, and to all who are afar off, as many as The Lord our God will call."*
>
> **Acts 2:39**

God has demonstrated that His Church needs His Power! Therefore, without this anointing of The Spirit of God, we cannot fulfil the mission of Christ today, just as they couldn't in their day!

"And Jesus came and spoke to them, saying, "All authority has been given to Me in heaven and on earth. Go therefore and make disciples of all the nations, baptizing them in the name of The Father and of the Son and of The Holy Spirit, teaching them to observe all things that I have commanded you; and lo, I am with you always, even to the end of the age." Amen.

Matthew 28: 18-20

Prayer

Help me, O Lord, to fulfil Your mission in my life!
I give myself to You this day and ask You to pour out Your Holy Spirit upon me!
Give me Your power to be a witness for You as You have declared in Your Word

Amen

Day 21a

Living in the Power and Realm of the

Holy Spirit

What does this mean to you? As a child of God recently saved by His Grace and forgiven, I desired to know God tangibly and realised there was the realm of The Holy Spirit to enable this! As far as I was concerned, without reality, there was no point!

At that time, I was a first-year student in London and had returned home to Derbyshire for the Easter vacation. The year was 1966, and I was nineteen years of age, coming on twenty. Initially, I knew very little of God's Word, and my only point of contact with God was God Himself through The Spirit! He had been real to me that evening as I sat in a small Pentecostal Church Hall alongside my mum. The Word I heard preached was used by God The Holy Spirit to open my eyes and lead me to repentance! I will describe my experience and describe what happened next.

I had attended Sunday School till I was twelve years old, so I should have had some knowledge of the Bible, but that did not happen in my case. But as far as the essentials go, I did not know anything about Jesus or what He had done!

I had no outside contact with anyone regarding the things of God. Therefore, I relied upon God guiding and directing me to the right places where I needed to be when I returned to London to continue studying at university. I began to read the Bible extensively. A small Collins Bible which I had received at Sunday School now became very useful! I became thirsty for more of God, and I needed to seek knowledge and get understanding.

The Bible was full of such Scriptures referring to "*thirst*" for Spiritual things:

"If anyone thirsts, let him come to Me and drink.
He who believes in Me, as the Scripture has said,
out of his heart will flow rivers of living water."
John 7:37

"Whoever drinks of this water will thirst again, but whoever drinks of the water that I shall give him will never thirst."
John 4:13-14

To be truthful, I remember how hesitant I was to pray openly within the church or speak to people about Christ.

Being in a Pentecostal church, I saw that many people demonstrated freedom and a love of The Lord in their lives that I couldn't replicate for myself. Some spoke in tongues and exercised verbal gifts of The Holy Spirit. Whenever they did, it brought a sense of awe with God's presence, which led me to seek The Lord Jesus about this according to the Scriptures. I remember being told that the word "baptise," meant to be *"fully immersed in"* as with water baptism, so I expected something special, total immersion in The Spirit of God!

> *"I (John the Baptist) indeed baptize you with water unto repentance, but He (Jesus) who is coming after me is mightier than I, whose sandals I am not worthy to carry. He will baptize you with The Holy Spirit and fire."*
> **Matthew 3:11**

> *"But you shall receive power when The Holy Spirit has come upon you; and you shall be witnesses to Me."* **Acts1:8**

Empowerment for Service

I sought this anointing of The Spirit with zeal and determination until I received it after being prayed for. I had a greater impetus to serve Him and speak of Him after this experience! The reality of God's love that I have for people increased whilst praise and worship entered a new dimension!

The liberty and freedom to speak of Christ, not by our oratory ability but by the unction of The Holy Spirit, is Divinely ordained to equip God's people to minister to the world His salvation through Jesus Christ! That is, God has made provision for His people to be effective and powerful witnesses.

We are called to be many things in the Scriptures but especially to be holy, self-controlled, walking with integrity, and in obedience to the Word of God. Jesus also requires this dynamic aspect in our lives to be effective in this world for Him. Unfortunately, it is this combination that is rare. Either the one is holy but has no or little power, or they have the power but are unholy, uncontrolled, and undisciplined in many cases! It is vital to appreciate the need to embrace this whole counsel of God! I need God's help and anointing to be bold, without fear to be an effective witness in the world, including signs!

The church's birth on the day of Pentecost coincided with the anticipated outpouring of The Spirit upon it, which confirms our need for The Spirit's empowerment in the church. If we are to complete the same mission today, He needs to be a dynamic, integral part of the life of every child of God! Jesus told the disciples to wait or tarry in Jerusalem until they received power from on high, so they must have needed this power! It follows that if they needed it, then we do too!

To understand this more fully, we need to look at The Holy Spirit's work in our lives at conversion to Jesus Christ and beyond to know how He operates. Whilst it is clear upon conversion that The Holy Spirit comes to dwell within us just as Jesus said – *"you must be born again,"* He The Spirit does not stop there! As we have seen on the Day of Pentecost, there is the separate phenomenon of being empowered by The Spirit to serve and witness, and we should follow Him ourselves for this same empowering!

Being born of The Spirit is a real work of God following our repentance, and we had no part in it! It is a miracle of Grace. However, The Spirit's anointing for service and empowerment is a different experience to be sought by the individual.

> *"Behold, I send the Promise of My Father upon you; but tarry in the city of Jerusalem until you are endued with power from on high."*
> **Luke 24:49**

Receiving The Spirit - Outward Manifestations

The book of Acts describes many experiences of receiving The Holy Spirit, and, in each case, it is an experiential occurrence that can be observed outwardly to others. Being born again is not like this!

For example, you believe and receive Jesus as your Saviour, and a miracle takes place; namely, The Spirit comes to dwell within you. If you should ask a person, *"Are you born again?"* and if the answer is *"Yes,"* this would infer that they have The Spirit within them. The action of The Holy Spirit, in this case, is primarily internal. In the book of Acts, however, the *receiving of The Holy Spirit* for empowerment is shown to display effects that are discernible or visible! In this case, the action of The Holy Spirit is mostly external!

Some had received Jesus and God's Word in the Bible, but so far, The Spirit had not fallen upon them! Paul talks about it this way when he asks,

> *"Did you receive The Spirit when you believed?"*
> **Acts 19:2**

> *"Now when the apostles who were at Jerusalem heard that Samaria had **received the word of God**, they sent Peter and John to them, who, when they had come down, prayed for them that they might receive The Holy Spirit. For, as yet, He had fallen upon none of them. **They had only been baptized in the name of The Lord Jesus**. Then they laid hands on them, and they received The Holy Spirit."*
> **Acts 8:14 –17**

Paul expects that a person who has "*received The Holy Spirit*" will know it as an experience when it happens.

> *Paul says,* **"Did you receive The Holy Spirit when you believed?"**

We scratch our heads and say, "I don't get it, Paul. If you assume we believed, why don't you assume we received The Holy Spirit? We've been taught that all who believe receive The Holy Spirit and that The Spirit is there whether there are any effects or not. But you talk as if there is a way to know we've received The Holy Spirit different from believing. You talk as if we could point to an experience of The Spirit apart from believing."

To answer your question, Paul asks,

"Did you receive The Spirit when you believed?"

He expects that a person who has *"received The Holy Spirit"* knows it, not just because it's an inference from his faith in Christ, but because it is an experience with effects to which we can point.
That is what runs through the book of Acts. All the explicit descriptions of receiving The Holy Spirit are experiential (not inferential).

Extract from A Resource by John Piper

"What Does It Mean to Receive The Holy Spirit?"

The fulfilment of the promise in Acts 1:8 shows that when The Spirit comes upon you, you will receive power, and through this power, you will be able to evangelize the world! This promise is made to everyone, and not just a few. The reason for this is so that in every generation, the Church may continue to grow!

Having tasted of the things of God, His Living Word, and the power of The Holy Spirit, my life could never be the same again! It is vital we know God's Word and read it, study it and love it because it is through this Word that The Spirit of God brings illumination to people! When God's Word becomes infused with The Spirit of God and is received into your life, the result is dynamite!

Upon reflection, I believe the following choices helped me:
- Die completely to self.
- Yield yourself unconditionally to do God's will for your life!
- God is a humble person, so – humble yourself!
- God is all-knowing, so - trust Him!
- God is Holy, truthful and righteous, so – believe and follow Him!
- God is reliable and true to His Word, so - learn of Him and keep His Word in your heart.

Notice how the above are all choices, and it is I that must make them! Things do not happen by themselves!

As we follow on to know The Lord, we have a spiritual guide within, The Holy Spirit, who can show us the way to go! Desiring to do God's will is the first step towards achieving it! God will always help us when we earnestly desire Him to work in our lives and show us His way.

Prayer

Thank You, Lord that You chose me from the beginning to love You, know You and Serve You until the end, and then live with You!

Thank You for your Grace by which I am saved.

Thank You, Jesus, for coming to this Earth and dying upon a cross for my sins. I decide today to choose Your way as my way.

Meditation

- *Let your focus in life be centred upon the person of Jesus Christ.*
- *Listen carefully to the Word of God preached.*
- *Afterwards, search the Scriptures to see if these things are so!*

"These were more fair-minded than those in Thessalonica, in that **they received the word with all readiness, and searched the Scriptures daily to find out whether these things were so.**"

Acts 17:11

Day 21b

His Purpose

Jesus' disciples needed equipping for the commission to preach The Gospel, and He told them to tarry at Jerusalem until they received power from on high. **So here we find the first significant role of The Holy Spirit in our lives – that of enduing us with boldness and Power.**

> *"Behold, I send the Promise of My Father upon you; but tarry in the city of Jerusalem until you are **endued with power from on high.**"*
> **Luke 24:49**

> *"But **you shall receive power when The Holy Spirit has come upon you**; and you shall be witnesses to Me in Jerusalem, and in all Judea and Samaria, and to the end of the earth."*
> **Acts 1:8**

The following is a quote from a well-known nineteenth-century Evangelist.

*"The great trouble with many of us is that we are working for God without power. We are sons of God - no doubt about that - and daughters of God, but we are sons and daughters without power. That is the trouble....**There are two ways in which The Holy Spirit comes to a man. The Spirit dwelling in him is one thing, and The Spirit on him for power is another thing**. I think that is where Christian people are misled. The trouble is, they are not looking for The Spirit of God for service. Our Gospel that we are preaching is a supernatural Gospel, and we have got to have supernatural power to preach it."*

Enduement For Service
D.L. Moody   1837 – 1899

The early disciples were with Jesus throughout His ministry and had the working of The Holy Spirit within them already. If Jesus said they needed the power to witness for Him, then surely, **we do too! Secondly, The Holy Spirit comes to each child of God as their Comforter and guide.** Jesus said He would pray to The Father, and He would send another Helper or Comforter. The disciples needed comfort in the absence of their Lord and would miss the companionship of Jesus to teach them and guide them. Here, Jesus re-assures them with the promise of The Holy Spirit, who would come to abide with them forever!

*"And I will pray The Father, and He will give you **another Helper**, that He may abide with you forever – The Spirit of truth..."*

John 14:16

The Greek for **"another helper"** is - *allos Parakletos*

allos - meaning "another of the **same kind**" – God The Holy Spirit

Parakletos - meaning "**helper or comforter**".

The following is relevant to this verse.

> *"What Jesus was to His disciples, so The Holy Spirit would be to His disciples. In His absence, Jesus said that The Holy Spirit was exactly like him, that is, equal with God.*
> *Indeed, that was the reason why the disciples were comforted – they knew that even though their comforter, master, and friend Jesus was leaving, another one who was exactly like him was going to take his place. He would comfort, counsel, help, intercede for, advocate for, strengthen, and be a stand-by support for them."* –

Extract: "Writings on Christian doctrine from a Pentecostal/Charismatic perspective."

As we have seen, Jesus referred to The Holy Spirit as the Comforter, but now we read another vital role He has. The Spirit of God has come to glorify Jesus, seeking to draw people to Him, convicting the world of sin, righteousness, and judgement. Jesus is always to be the centre and focus! Furthermore, we are the recipients of The Holy Spirit's illumination, revealing both Christ and the Word of God to us.

"However, when He, The Spirit of truth, has come, He will guide you into all truth; for He will not speak on His own authority, but whatever He hears He will speak; and He will tell you things to come. **He will glorify Me, for He will take of what is Mine and declare it to you.***"*
John 16:13-14

I think that a good guide when hearing a message preached is this – "to what extent do we hear the name of Jesus mentioned?" Was Jesus directly or indirectly the focus and primary purpose of the message?

We must never forget that The Gospel of Jesus Christ is a simple message of good news and we do well never to depart from this fact. It should always be a joyous time whenever talking about Jesus and God's salvation through Him! What a blessing! How encouraging to know that Jesus used ordinary, simple, mostly uneducated people to preach and share The Gospel and empowered them to do so!

The point here is that Jesus did not esteem it a requirement to be learned and educated to do His work, only that we should come to Him believing and be born again! We can easily forget this and get it wrong!

Always remember that God loves you as a person and not for what you know or don't know. It must be said that I hardly knew any of God's Word at the age of nineteen when I came to Christ! I heard the Word preached, I was convicted of The Holy Spirit, and I received Christ! Thereafter, I began by knowing the reality of God's presence and was hungry for the Word of God. God loves to bless us with His salvation just as we are and, afterwards, teach and instruct us in His Word and guide us through life Himself!

This idea reminds me of something I heard in my workplace! I taught at a Furthermore Education College in London for 37 years, and at the beginning of the academic year, when it was enrolment time, some students would seek advice regarding their choice of subjects when applying for admission on the A level Course. Well, those who were prospective Law students had a surprise! The relevant lecturers in Law would often stress that it was unnecessary to study A-Level Law if you wished to take up Law at University but instead choose three good subjects that would prove their ability to research and learn! Universities tend to prefer teaching you about Law themselves - right from scratch!

The Bible says that God loves us just as we are! All He requires is that we are willing to come to Him, receive Him and learn of Him! What a blessing that is!

There was something that made the disciples of Jesus stand out, and it was the power and authority Jesus imparted to them through The Holy Spirit! Their knowledge and understanding of God and the Scriptures seemed to take off exponentially from the Day of Pentecost! It is the same today! People cannot understand where we get our knowledge of Jesus. They fail to appreciate how you can say you know Jesus as a person and why you read the Bible!

I cannot emphasise enough the importance of those Scriptures that teach us fundamental truths about The Holy Spirit. It is true to say that if we become filled with The Holy Spirit, we ought to be filled with Jesus Christ and love His Word and vice-versa! It is a joyous experience, or as the Bible puts it,

> *"Though now you do not see Him, yet believing, you rejoice with **joy inexpressible and full of glory."***
>
> **1 Peter 1:8**

Upon becoming born again, there was a particular transformation in my life. Whereas previously, I very much disliked the sound of Hymns and hearing people speak about Jesus and the Bible, suddenly I now loved to listen to the pastor talk about Jesus and sing songs and Hymns in church! To experience this change was a blessing.

Soon after I had been baptised in The Holy Spirit, an occasion arose at a University Christian Union function that I attended. The meeting was continually interrupted by a rough man off the streets who seemed drunk, which completely dampened the atmosphere with a tenseness that could be cut with a carving knife! People were invited to answer this man who was ridiculing faith in God, but no one did. All were afraid to do so! You could hear a pin drop!

After a while, seeing that no one spoke, I felt compelled to stand up and challenge the mocking onlooker! Faces were downcast all around looking glum, but being moved upon by The Spirit of God, I stood up and gave my testimony of how I came to have faith in Jesus. I found that once I had committed myself to stand and speak, the words that came out of my mouth flowed easily like a gushing stream of living water! I knew The Spirit of God was inspiring my words. There was someone else besides myself involved, and I knew it was a manifestation of The Holy Spirit that gave me boldness to speak! I had no inhibition, no fear, and no embarrassment, so much so that I could hardly remember what I had said later that evening! The room was liberated into release and freedom with praise to God from my fellow peers and the intruder; well, he just shut up and became speechless!

As I was leaving that meeting, a Ph.D. student walked over to me, looking quite aghast and shaken, and said,

> *"How did you learn to speak like that?*
> *I wish I could speak in that way!*
> *It just flowed effortlessly.*

It was amazing!"

That was the first occasion that I had experienced the demonstration and power of The Holy Spirit to witness for Jesus in a public setting. The Ph.D. student had mistakenly imagined that I had a gift for speaking, but I knew what had happened! It had nothing to do with me, only that I had to stand up, ignore my embarrassment, say something, and then The Holy Spirit took over!

Like the Ph.D. student, we can also get it wrong! We fail to realise that this can be The Spiritual norm for a born-again believer, and, indeed, it is meant to be! Instead, we can struggle, battling with our fears and reservations, which was not my experience, neither was it that of Peter on the Day of Pentecost as he boldly challenged the crowd bearing in mind that the *natural Peter* was very much afraid at one time and denied Christ! Do we get this? Do we realise that which is flesh is flesh, and that which is Spirit is Spirit!? God does not want us to operate in the flesh but the power and unction of The Spirit! Therefore, God gives us His Spirit for this very reason!

Room for Thought

*"Now when the apostles at Jerusalem heard that Samaria had **received the word of God**, they sent to them Peter and John, who came Down and prayed for them that they might receive*

The Holy Spirit; for it had not yet fallen on any of them, but they had only been baptized in the name of The Lord Jesus. Then they laid their hands on them and they received The Holy Spirit."

Acts 8: 14-17

Meditation

"For God has not given us a spirit of fear, but of power and of love and of a sound mind."
2 Timothy 1:7

Day 22

The Spirit Bestows His Gifts

> *"Now concerning spiritual gifts, brethren, I do not want you to be ignorant... There are diversities of gifts, but the same Spirit. There are differences of ministries, but the same Lord. And there are diversities of activities, but it is the same God who works all in all."*
> **1 Corinthians 12:1, 4-7**

This subject is of particular interest to me! To answer why we must go back to the very beginning when I was first challenged about The Lord by my mother!

At this time, I had not long arrived home from University on vacation. One morning having just come down the stairs from my bedroom, I ventured into the living room and was completely taken by surprise to see mum sat in front of the open coal fire reading her Bible! Upon observation, a moment of up-surging embarrassment and contempt rose to the surface within me! I was feeling superior and full of pride. It all seemed to be an odd situation. In a sarcastic manner and conceited tone of voice, I blurted out to my mother and said,

"I believe that if there is a God, then He would be real; He would talk to you and You with Him! All this getting dressed up and going to church on a Sunday and then coming home to be the same, it is all hypocrisy to me!"

Surprisingly, my mum reacted oppositely to that which I expected. Instead of being provoked by my rash words into saying something defensive or argumentative, she looked at me, smiled then said,

"That's exactly what we believe down at church!"

The conversation ended at that. I was partly impressed by mum's answer, for she seemed to be agreeing with me despite my arrogance and criticism! Even so, I was challenged by this experience; it was the beginning of many.

I had no desire at that point in my life to become Religious – if ever! I was not interested – full stop! I understand now that it takes a miracle for a person to believe in The Lord; a miracle of Grace, and that's what happened to me!

The following is *"my testimony"* of how I came to The Lord as a nineteen-year-old student. It was God's time for me, and I could never have foreseen that it was to be my time also! Having ventured into a church, I came out a different person to when I went in! Unknown to me that evening, I was to have a spiritual encounter and experience what was to change my life forever!

My Testimony

At the age of nineteen, I was living at home with my parents in a place called Langwith Junction in Derbyshire, England, which, as the name suggests, was a railway junction with sheds full of steam engines. It was a small village about one mile away from Shirebrook, a coal-mining market town.

By now, I was well into university studies at Chelsea College of Science, London, and I always looked forward to coming home during vacation times to see my then-girlfriend Pauline Marchant, who lived about seven miles away in Mansfield. She was awesome, and I considered myself very lucky!

During one Easter vacation in 1966, I was ill in bed with the flu at my mum's house. I remember feeling quite low. My mother asked me to come to church with her as she said I would feel much better if I did. With it being a dark, cold Wednesday evening, I reluctantly yielded to her pressure, feeling I had no option but to go. At least it was dark outside, and no one would see me and where I was going! You see, I felt stupid and embarrassed going to a church.

Upon arrival at a medium-sized Pentecostal Church hall in Shirebrook, I saw no one there except two or three very elderly people - my mum didn't tell me it was a Prayer Meeting! To my utter amazement, I recognised the man who stood at the front; it was Archie Roberts, and he owned a Fish and Chip shop in town!

I sat down sheepishly near the front, feeling very conspicuous and downcast. Soon Archie began to preach, having read out a verse or two from the Bible previously. He had read the passage from **Matthew 16: 24-26**, which says,

"Then Jesus said to His disciples, "If anyone desires to come after Me, let him deny himself, and take up his cross, and follow Me. For whoever desires to save his life will lose it, but whoever loses his life for My sake will find it. For what profit is it to a man if he gains the whole world, and loses his own soul? Or what will a man give in exchange for his soul?"

He talked about a man being born into this world naked with nothing and leaving it in a similar fashion. I was always inspired by truth, and I could not dispute this – it was true!

As he went on about life, the word began to speak to me – "what would it profit me if I were to gain all the riches in the world only to die and then - that's it? I would leave everything behind!" As a student, I had plans to live a "full life", hopefully with a good job, but this word I was hearing shook me up to think more deeply and seriously - what was the meaning and purpose of my life? Where was I going? What was after?

Being prompted by mum's elbow, I stood up at the end of the meeting to walk out to the front for prayer and to give my life to JESUS CHRIST.

Upon returning home, I knew something spiritual had taken place that evening in the little hall; in fact, something supernatural! I had walked into the hall not knowing anything about God, but I walked out knowing this,

"GOD is VERY REAL."

I knew because somehow, I had just met with HIM!! - Like I said, something spiritual happened - I don't know how - but it did!

God has been real and personal to me from that day forward to this very day, some fifty-five years later. I had once said mockingly to my mum that if God is real, then He should talk with us, and for that matter, we with Him!

I instantly became hungry to read the Bible. I got to know Him more and more through His Word, which was opened to me by His in-dwelling Holy Spirit! He gave me what I was looking for, a purpose and reason for life but importantly, a real, living relationship with God. I was not interested in religion, but knowing God for myself - that was very different! Now, I know this life is not the end but that it goes on with Him FOREVER!

It was the beginning of many conscious supernatural experiences in my life. I could not stop reading the Bible and praying to God! I attended every church meeting! The things of The Spirit were very real to me thus far, and there was more to come!

Regarding spiritual gifts, these followed my conversion quickly, and I include a list of them as stated in the Bible.

> "But the manifestation of The Spirit is given to each one for the profit of all: for to one is given **the word of wisdom** through The Spirit, to another **the word of knowledge** through the same Spirit to another **faith** by the same Spirit, to another **gifts of healings** by the same Spirit, to another the **working of miracles**, to another **prophecy**, to another **discerning of spirits**, to another **different kinds of tongues**, to another **the interpretation of tongues**. But one and the same Spirit works all these things, distributing to each one individually as He wills."
>
> **1 Corinthians 12: 7-11**

In some churches, including the church at Corinth in the Scriptures, the operation of these gifts proved problematic! As you can imagine, people are greatly aroused emotionally when The Spirit manifests Himself! He is not the author of confusion, but we sometimes can be! Unfortunately, this has caused some churches to move away from the gifts of The Spirit, rather like *throwing the baby out with the bath water*!

My church, being Pentecostal, meant that I observed gifts of The Spirit operating in meetings. I would search the Bible to find where it mentioned such gifts and became enlightened! Their operation in the church had an edifying effect showing me that God was real and *in this place*, which appealed to me. It was as if God was showing me,

> "Yes, I am real, and I speak to you personally as you desired!".

I always liked to hear a message in tongues followed by the interpretation because it impacted me so much that God could be so real and speak in such a way! Whilst the interpretations were not infallible, for no words can supersede the Word of God, they were inspirational, a sort of affirmative message associated with the Word of God that had just been preached, focusing upon specifics. So I would listen intently *"to what The Spirit was saying to the church."*

I realised that the Word of God preached was God's Word to us and not the words of a man and that this fact was being authenticated in our midst by The Spirit Himself.

I had a great thirst within me. It was God The Holy Spirit that was at work in my life. Every time I prayed it was,

> *Lord, I thirst for You; fill me with Yourself! I want to know you more! I want more of You!*

People must have been tired of me praying the same thing repeatedly, but that was the way it was! I was bringing an enormous vessel before the Throne of Grace to be filled, and I couldn't stop. God continually invites all to come to Him, and I intend to be one of them!

Over the years, however, I soon discovered different churches believe different things, and not all are born-again believers! Some disregard the gifts of The Spirit entirely for various reasons, to my disbelief and shock!

In a sense, the reality of the world kicked in! My initial bubble had seemingly burst! I needed to learn to accept all people irrespective of their individual beliefs. There were many people out there and not all the same as me! However, God had done a work in me, which I was never to forget irrespective of all else. Consequently, I learned to walk alone with God, especially at work where few, if any, believed. Therefore, I always kept close to God and His Word, and He kept me.

Time and time again, I would look back with gratitude to how I began with The Lord in such a simple and uncomplicated manner in an unassuming little church of mostly elderly folk and then think,

> *"I thank God I was totally free from any religious hang-ups, or set beliefs at the beginning; that I knew absolutely nothing about anything in the religious world and its teachings but instead was new, fresh and alive knowing Jesus Christ as my Lord and Saviour ...and in a real and living way."*

It was God who had called me and put inside of me the desire to know Him and His Word fervently. He showed me just how real He was, as if responding to my heart's cry for reality when as yet I did not believe or know Him! I love God! I was transformed in my thinking towards Him and simply could not fully take in just how real He was to me personally! How I had been so wrong! I had been totally blind before and dead to the things of The Spirit, but now – I had been made alive!

> *"And you He made alive, who were dead in trespasses and sins, in which you once walked according to the course of this world,* according to the prince of the power of the air, The Spirit who now works in the sons of disobedience ... But God, who is rich in mercy, because of His great love with which He loved us, ***even when we were dead in trespasses, made us alive together with Christ...***"
>
> **Ephesians 2:1,2,4**

The result was that I had become thirsty and hungry. The Spirit illuminated His Word giving me understanding as I read, studied and heard it expounded.

Later, Spiritual truths sometimes came as pictures whereby I could see the whole idea of what God was showing me from the Word. I knew God's Word had to be real, living, practical and edifying to others, and I believe this was my mission for life to make it just that!

Since leaving University, I worked in a College of Furthermore Education as a lecturer. Soon, I discovered that my understanding of God's Word and the liberty of The Holy Spirit enabled me to testify, to all, of my Faith in Jesus Christ!

As mentioned, I had initially attended a small humble Assemblies of God Pentecostal church where I learnt all about Spiritual gifts right from the start. I knew nothing else, and it suited me very well! Why? Because Holy Spirit's presence and the Word of God together brought great enlightenment of truth about God! People in those earlier days operated gifts respectfully and orderly especially Speaking in Tongues. I immediately desired to be filled with The Holy Spirit to obtain the boldness promised. I prayed for God to fill me and baptise me in The Holy Spirit, and He did!

I witnessed boldly at University to all my colleagues, and some kept their distance from me after that, but God gave me new friends in the college Christian Union. I had received the power to witness according to the Scriptures. I soon operated gifts as moved upon by The Holy Spirit, firstly on the University campus then in church meetings.

A favourite Scripture of mine is when Jesus spoke out to the crowd on the last day of the Feast of Tabernacles.

He cried out, saying, "On the last day, that great day of the feast, Jesus stood and cried out, saying, "If anyone thirsts, let him come to Me and drink. He who believes in Me, as the Scripture has said, out of his heart will flow rivers of living water." **But this He spoke concerning The Spirit, whom those believing in Him would receive; for The Holy Spirit was not yet given because Jesus was not yet glorified."**

John 7: 37-39

It was Jesus that heralded in the Power of The Holy Spirit upon the early church. It was well accepted and understood that those who believed in Jesus and were born-again of The Spirit could also receive the Power to be witnesses and have gifts that would emanate from The Spirit upon whoever He chose.

> *"And these signs shall follow them that believe; In my name* **(Jesus)** *shall they cast out devils;* **they shall speak with new tongues... they shall lay hands on the sick, and they shall recover."*
> **Mark 16:17-18b**

> *"I* **(John the Baptist)** *indeed baptize you with water unto repentance, but He who is coming after me is mightier than I, whose sandals I am not worthy to carry.* **He will baptize you with The Holy Spirit and fire."**
> **Matthew 3:11**

Interestingly, the Greek word for *power* in this verse is **Dunamis,** from which we derive the word *dynamite!* It is a supernatural ability received in its entirety by The Spirit of God!

What are Spiritual Gifts for?

The gifts empower us with supernatural abilities to edify the church and evangelise the world. Their purpose is to build up the Kingdom and not the flesh!

Today, more than ever, we need a continual fresh anointing of The Holy Spirit to strengthen and encourage God's people. We are living in dark times. Even as I write this book, the world is experiencing a pandemic; a pestilence, as our Lord prophesied would come to pass in the last days

The preaching of The Gospel of the Kingdom is and always will be the primary commission from our Lord, and the gifts of The Spirit are a powerful means of delivering it! People need God's life, a new heart and reality, not religion! Therefore, the power and presence of The Holy Spirit in our daily lives is something for which we are to seek and thirst.

Here are some important truths of wisdom to consider and take to heart that I have personally learned over 55 years as a born-again believer, mostly in a spirit-filled church environment.

- *The operation of Spiritual gifts by a person* **does not signify or indicate any bearing whatsoever upon their spiritual standing and holiness before The Lord.**
- *Operating Spiritual gifts* **has no bearing whatsoever upon the person's character.** *Character can only improve as a person yields to the process of being sanctified by God's Word and Spirit, which takes place over a long time, indeed, a lifetime.*
- **No person has any power whatsoever of themselves to perform miracles through the operation of any Spiritual gift.** *Power belongs to God. In fact, the person praying, for example, is often unconscious of anything happening and operates entirely by faith.*

- *The **greatest miracle** and gift a person can ever experience occurs when they become **born-again into God's Kingdom, which** provides eternal life! All other miracles are transitory, having no eternal value.*

So, The Holy Spirit, as mentioned, bestows His spiritual gifts upon and within each believer, but this is not necessarily automatic. We must also play alongside The Holy Spirit by being obedient to God's Word and thirsting for more of God. Even so, God knows us more than we do ourselves, just of what we are capable. He will ultimately bless us according to His purposes as we focus upon Jesus. Remember!

The empowerment of The Spirit to witness is for every born-again believer.

Are we ready and desirous for this?

Conclusion

In the past, many people have concentrated on the gifts more than the Giver! They have changed, to their detriment, the central feature of meetings to manifestations and operations of The Spirit instead of keeping the focus upon Jesus and preaching the Word.

The gifts and their operations are to edify and build up the church, which is the Biblical stance. Whilst this is the case, we should always balance this seeking to give the greatest pre-eminence and focus upon preaching and teaching the Word of God, making provision for the Whole Counsel of God. Let us also remember, rather than discard, that we cannot exclude or ignore our dynamic position with Christ through The Spirit! We are what Christ has made us, that is, seated with Him in the heavenly places, and as such, we need to share His power and authority in our earthly mission to propagate The Gospel!

Human choice, the flesh, and probably fear have made this a difficult proposition to fulfil for many in the Church who seemingly do not have the liberty and freedom to serve Christ in power! Yes, our life in Christ is to be Godly, devoted, and disciplined. The Biblical pattern we are to adhere to also includes being dynamic through the overflowing of The Spirit acting powerfully, which is often missing and most needful today. More than ever, if God's people are to walk in power and victory!

Prayer

I thank You, Lord, for saving me by dying upon the cross for all of my sins.

I desire greater reality in my life of Yourself and Your presence that I might know You more intimately.

I come to You, Lord Jesus. I ask You to fill me with The Holy Spirit and Power in accordance with Your Word [1]. *I desire to have boldness to speak about You.*

"I indeed baptize you with water unto repentance, but He who is coming after me is mightier than I, whose sandals I am not worthy to carry. **He will baptize you with The Holy Spirit and fire."**

Matthew 3:11

Day 23

Walking in The Spirit - 1

"If we live in The Spirit, let us also walk in The Spirit."
Galatians 5:25

Our personal communion and relationship with God are most important, and this opening verse is paramount, perhaps more so than we might first imagine! Walking with God in The Spirit naturally, or should I say supernaturally, involves everything to do with our new life in Christ. It includes our understanding of God's Word, our obedience, commitment, dedication and consecration, as well as the submission and yielding of our will to doing God's will and purposes! All are fulfilled in this verse, ***"walk in The Spirit!"*** Only by The Holy Spirit can we live and function in the way God requires of us to, and without Him, we are dead to the things of God! His voice, guidance, illumination of God's Word and empowerment, are but a few of the many qualities and functions essential for each one of us. He is the one who will take the Word of God and show us how to live! He is the one who will guide us and take us through life!

We must understand the word "*walk*" in the above verse. The Greek literally means:

" to walk in line with"

So, if we place this literal meaning into the verse we read, "If we live in The Spirit, let us also ***walk in line with*** The Spirit."

To illustrate this, imagine you are walking down a straight path where you are to look neither to the left or to the right but to walk straight ahead step by step allowing The Spirit of God to guide you. You are always to **walk or keep in line with The Spirit** for success and safety! He knows the pit-falls that lie ahead, the dangers, the unwise decisions, the choices that could easily divert or distract you and the temptations of the flesh. In short, The Spirit knows the best and wisest road to walk down, but we do not.

We need to walk in The Spirit when it comes to our dealing with money. God knows what we need, what takes priority, and how we should manage our money, but this takes commitment and trust in God. We shall see later in the book that for God to have full jurisdiction over our finances, we need to consider tithing to Him, for the Bible says this is how to walk with God when it comes to money! Many people find this a 'big one'!

One of the greatest dilemmas facing the younger generation today is their attitude towards money, though it is not exclusively a young person's problem. For example, the popular trend of borrowing money to buy things! It is not considered borrowing money today as it has a more respectable face called a credit card! Nevertheless, using a credit card and not paying the total sum off at the end of the month is essentially borrowing money and charged with interest!

Today, it is more acceptable to spend money than saving it, which is virtually unheard of! It is more common to borrow money than to put it aside until you have enough! The driving force is the compulsion to buy now rather than wait! It is far more convenient to obtain those things you perceive are needful by taking out a loan. This attitude quickly identifies with that of the world's way of thinking! It is feeding the desires of the flesh and not The Spirit. Because at heart, the focus is upon material things. You end up living for the pleasures and comforts of this world and fail to give to God what is rightfully His! You become so self-orientated by what money can give you that Godly qualities such as giving and being generous become absent in your thinking! A common word to describe this attitude is selfishness. Perhaps worst of all, you reap what you have sown and end up in debt!

It would help if you asked yourself the following questions. Do I really need certain items? Are they essential and necessary? To avoid excess monthly outgoings, why not wait until you can afford to purchase them at a later date? In reality, those commodities of interest are not usually that important. Do you need an exotic luxury holiday abroad or a larger T.V. set when the old is just fine or a car change because you desire a trendier one when the one you have is running perfectly well! We are not talking here about needing a new sweeper, washing machine, or other essential domestic items; instead, we are thinking about all those things that are not critical, as mentioned! Do you see a difference?

It is this materialistic, covetous and selfish attitude that deviates some people away from today's subject.

Walking in The Spirit

To walk in The Spirit is to **walk in line with the Word of God.** The Word reveals a different attitude towards money when compared with that of the world. Consider the following Scripture.

> *"Do not lay up for yourselves treasures on earth, where moth and rust destroy and where thieves break in and steal; but lay up for yourselves treasures in heaven, where neither moth nor rust destroys and where thieves do not break in and steal. **For where your treasure is, there your heart will be also."***
> **Matthew 6:19-21**

We can easily lose track of the fact that everything in this world is transient and temporary! God's priority is always to prepare us to do His good works and live for Eternity. These Scriptures serve as balance! We need to remember who we are, where we are, and what our purpose is! Following the crowd is not an option. We live in a fallen world, our real home is in Heaven, and our old nature, the flesh, will trifle with the world given half a chance!

As God's children, the first requirement is to learn to walk in The Spirit, in line with the Word of God. If you move off the pathway that God has ordained for you to walk in as outlined in His Word, you are no longer walking in line with The Spirit but doing things your own way. By not seeking God's opinion in all of your choices, you will inevitably end up in trouble, or things will simply not work out as well as they could have done. Why? Because you were leaning upon your own understanding and choosing to walk your own way. My prayer is,

> *"Oh! That we might trust The Lord with our every decision and not be afraid to allow Him full reign and control over all our life!"*

The following Scripture is very well-known but is it well adhered to!?

> *"Trust in The Lord with all your heart, And **lean not on your own understanding;**
> **In all your ways acknowledge Him**, And He shall direct your paths."*
> **Proverbs 3:5-6**

The irony is we so often say we believe in the Scriptures and know them well. We have heard numerous sermons preached, but we don't practice what we hear or take them sufficiently to heart to apply them. It is just as if we had never known them! When trouble arrives, we find ourselves unable to know what to do, having lost the habit of consulting The Lord because we have not previously been walking in line with The Spirit and adhering to those attitudes revealed in Scripture.

Let us seek to remedy this so that it need never be a problem! Let us begin walking in line with The Holy Spirit! Let us ask The Lord to help us.

> *"Show me Your ways, O Lord;*
> *Teach me Your paths.*
> *Lead me in Your truth and teach me."*
> **Psalm 25:4-5**

This morning Let's address the problem! Let's focus upon the role of The Holy Spirit in our lives so that we can genuinely say, "I am walking in line with The Spirit!"

Below are some questions that are likely to be relevant.

- *Am I comfortable in allowing The Spirit of God to show me His ways or do I feel this can infringe upon my own plans and choices?*
- *Am I in tune with The Holy Spirit every day or just sometimes?*

It must be said that the subject today is easily put on the back burner. You can be filled with The Spirit, exercising the gifts, be in a senior position in a church, but that does not imply that you are automatically walking in line with The Spirit, especially when it comes to money! The latter, which is sadly missing, is a choice of submission to The Spirit that you need to take.

Jesus was *going away,* so He went to great lengths to introduce The Holy Spirit to His followers when He told them,

> *"However, when He, The Spirit of truth, has come, He will guide you into all truth; for He will not speak on His own authority, but whatever He hears He will speak; and He will tell you things to come. He will glorify Me, for He will take of what is Mine and declare it to you."*
>
> **John 16: 13-14**

- *What do you make of this passage – in reality?*
- *Is it a statement only and nothing else or have you proved each detail to be true in your personal experience?*
- *Do you know the presence of the Holy Spirit in your day-to-day life?*
- *Are you conscious within of His moving's in your life where God is seeking to tell you which way to go and not to go?*

The simplest way to look at this subject today is to look at it simply! Think about it! If I have The Holy Spirit abiding within me, He will speak to me just as Jesus said He would.

- *He will guide you into all truth*
- *Whatever He hears, He will speak*
- *He will tell you things to come*
- *He will take of what is Mine and declare it to you.*

> *The Spirit Himself bears witness with our spirit* that we are children of God
> **Romans 8:16**

Pause for a moment to reflect upon the above statements of Jesus. The question, first and foremost, you need to ask yourself before God is this,

"Do I believe this? Do I want this intimacy and control of The Spirit in my personal life, or am I afraid to do so for some reason?"

Why is it that some of us struggle to walk in line with The Spirit if He is alive within us and has been sent to help and direct us? This big question requires us to search our hearts. Yes, He is there, but as always, The Holy Spirit waits for our choices to be in line with what is right according to the Word of God. In such cases, if The Spirit's promptings go unheeded, if, indeed, The Spirit moves upon our lives and we quench Him, then will we not inevitably feel guilty and lose our peace with God? Ultimately, if we persist in going our own way, The Spirit will likely turn away for a season until we are willing to hear and respond with obedience to God's way according to the written Word of God It can take days, weeks, months and even years, but God is faithful! The tragedy is that we miss all that God has for us while seeking to enjoy the pleasures of life! We can miss His calling, having replaced it with our own agenda.

It may seem unbelievable, but it is true! We can begin with God, receiving His goodness by accepting Christ as our Saviour and obtaining eternal life, but to go any furthermore with God proves difficult to our flesh. *I didn't sign up for this!*

Jesus spoke of and included this attitude in the parable of the sower.

> *"Now he who received seed among the thorns is he who hears the word, and the cares of this world and* ***the deceitfulness of riches choke the word, and he becomes unfruitful."***
> **Matthew 13: 22**

So, God in His love waits until I will receive Him as Lord over my whole life as well as Saviour! Only God knows the outcome of such situations!

Let us meditate and take to heart the opening Scripture for today.

> *"If we live in The Spirit, let us also walk in The Spirit."*
>
> **Galatians 5:25**

That is, let us endeavour to walk in line with The Spirit by walking in line with the Word of God!

Let us pray:

Forgive me, Lord, for not confiding in You and listening to Your still small voice!

I now know how much I have done things according to my own choices, in my own strength, and not according to Your Word.

I now realise why I have been feeling so low and not at peace!

I see clearly from Scripture that having accepted and believing in You that You are abiding in my heart.

I come to You now repentant, asking You to forgive me. I desire to come and obey You in the future from this day forth.

Be my strength, O Lord, and lead me by Your Holy Spirit in accordance to Your Word.

Amen

Day 24

Walking in The Spirit - 2

*"I say then: **Walk in The Spirit**, and you shall not fulfil the lust of the flesh."*
Galatians 5:16

On DAY 7, titled *"Flesh"*, we saw, in Scripture, that the word *flesh* is primarily used as a metaphor to describe sinful tendencies. In such cases, it would refer to man's sinful human nature acquired at birth. Furthermoremore, we looked at the verse below to see how we must no longer walk according to the flesh but according to The Spirit.

*"There is therefore now no condemnation to those who are in Christ Jesus, who do not walk according to the flesh, but **according to The Spirit.**"*
Romans 8:1

On DAY 12, titled *"The Flesh and The Spirit"*, we saw that to walk according to the flesh is to follow the sinful desires of one's old life, whereas to walk according to The Spirit is to follow The Holy Spirit and to live in a way pleasing to Him.

> *"For those who live according to the flesh set their minds on the things of the flesh, but those who live according to The Spirit, the things of The Spirit."*
>
> **Romans 8:5**

Once again, our focus is on walking in The Spirit. However, this time, we shall look at how The Holy Spirit, who dwells in our heart, always seeks to draw us away from the things of the flesh.

First, we will remind ourselves that God The Holy Spirit plays a central inward role by living in our hearts, which God designed to create a love for Him and His Word as we walk intimately in submission and obedience to His leading. In short, God has demonstrated how much He desires the heart of man to be surrendered over to Him as it is written,

> *"Behold,* **You desire truth in the inward parts, And in the hidden part You will make me to know wisdom."**
>
> **Psalm 51:6**

Next, we look at the New Covenant that Jesus spoke of, in His Blood, and which The Holy Spirit signified in the Book of Hebrews, quoting from Jeremiah 31: 31-33

> *"This is the covenant that I will make with them after those days, says The Lord:* **I will put My laws into their hearts, and in their minds, I will write them..."**
>
> **Hebrews 10:16**

The new birth, which we experience through believing in Christ, has initiated our entry into this New Covenant with God. Jesus made this possible only because of the redeeming, cleansing power of His shed blood. The New Covenant points to the new work of the indwelling Holy Spirit who becomes operative within us. "Writing" the law of God on our hearts is the great work of The Holy Spirit! When you believe that The Spirit is real, that He is alive in you, you can allow Him to guide you in every choice and decision.

Our bodies are now called the temple of The Holy Spirit, and we are not our own, but we belong to God. Once again, this is because Jesus has purchased us with the redeeming power of His own blood, making us His possession! The temple of God resides in the hearts of His people, and The Holy Spirit, Himself, has moved in!

> *"Or do you not know that your body is the temple of The Holy Spirit who is in you, whom you have from God, and you are not your own?"*
> **1 Corinthians 6:19**

Jesus foretold this phenomenon to the woman of Samaria,

> *"But the hour is coming, and now is, when the* ***true worshipers will worship The Father in spirit and truth; for The Father is seeking such to worship Him. God is Spirit, and those who worship Him must worship in spirit and truth."***
> **John 4: 23-24**

The Spirit of God has come to reside in us for a purpose! What had failed before will now succeed! The Scriptures describe it as "Christ in you the hope of Glory!"

> "To them God willed to make known what are the riches of the glory of this mystery among the Gentiles: which is Christ in you, the hope of glory."
> **Colossians 1:27**

In the Old Testament, attempting to live by God's law was problematic, not only because it could never make the people perfect but because, by its very nature, they had to adhere to a list of external commandments. Obeying a law of commandments written on parchment or stone is not as effective as obeying a Person who lives inside you, showing you the right way and the wrong way! The following Scripture points out that now you can fulfil God's will through the inner influence of The Holy Spirit instead of the outer result of the law of God.

> "For what the law could not do in that it was weak through the flesh, God did by sending His own Son in the likeness of sinful flesh, on account of sin: He condemned sin in the flesh, **that the righteous requirement of the law might be fulfilled in us who do not walk according to the flesh but according to The Spirit."**
> **Romans 8: 3-4**

Walking in The Spirit is paramount and essential to the child of God. We are not under the law but grace, and this is how it works in practice, by walking in line with The Spirit! God, The Holy Spirit, thinks in line with all the righteousness of God in Christ. Indeed Jesus said,

> *"...when He, The Spirit of truth, has come, He will guide you into all truth...He will glorify Me, for He will take of what is Mine and declare it to you."*
> **John 16: 13-14**

Because it is personal, we can set our minds on the things of The Spirit, and in so doing, He will guide us, but if we do not set our minds upon The Spirit through our submission and choice, how can He guide us into all truth? It's as simple as that! The Law works by compulsion, but Grace works through love and choice!
The food of The Spirit is the Word of God which He, Himself, inspired men to write down, so the more you read and know the Word, the more He can guide you into all truth! The Spirit of God will never deviate from the written Word of God, but the beauty is that what you learn from The Spirit will always help and clarify the Word of God, giving deeper meaning and insight that will be personal and relevant to you!

Understand that the insight and knowledge of The Spirit of God far exceed your own; after all, He is the Eternal Spirit with The Father and the Son, and He, it is that abides within you! The Spirit within will seek to show you the right way from the wrong way.

The *"wrong way"* is not necessarily a way of sin. Rather, because God sees the outcome of each decision, The Holy Spirit will wish to lead us upon the best pathway with the best outcome that will always bring glory to God. We need faith and trust in The Lord and, of course, our obedience to do this.

Having, therefore, briefly looked at the background to the work and function of The Holy Spirit working in us, we now move to the real life-long battle that takes place within us. It is The Spirit versus the flesh! Some have called it the battlefield of the mind!

> ***"I say then: Walk in The Spirit, and you shall not fulfil the lust of the flesh. For the flesh lusts against The Spirit, and The Spirit against the flesh; and these are contrary to one another…"***
>
> **Galatians 5: 16-17**

Here is the conflict that exists! We ought to expect the battle, for two diametrically opposed natures live within the same body. One is essentially a fallen nature controlled by the enemy from birth and a slave to sin, while the second is born from above under God's control living in the temple of The Holy Spirit.

Our victory over the flesh is made possible by Christ and His death upon the cross! As we receive Christ, the victor over sin and the devil, we receive His power to put to death the things of the flesh. The Bible puts it like this,

> *"... if Christ be in you, the body is dead because of sin; but The Spirit is life because of righteousness."*
>
> **Romans 8: 10**

The enemy has no power over us because the Blood of Jesus has broken the power of sin that it should no longer rule and have dominion over us! The Devil knows this, so we, by faith in God's Word, must overcome his temptations, lies and accusations causing the conflict!

We must learn to do our part, not with our human strength or willpower but with God's power and the authority of His Word. As we speak the Word of God, in faith, demons flee! As we proclaim that, of ourselves, we are unworthy and that our righteousness is solely through the Blood of Jesus, the enemy cannot condemn us. We are the righteousness of God in Christ! God has redeemed us and accepted us through the Blood of Jesus, and we now belong to Him![1]

Understand that the war between Good and evil is over! Christ won the victory at the cross! All heaven is aware of this! Every evil spirit is aware of this, but the battles still rage, and we must stand against the enemy of our souls and assert our position in Christ from the written Word of God.[1]

[1] *"Living Victoriously in the Last days"* Brian Reddish

Meditation

The Bible says,

*"Therefore, submit to God. **Resist the devil and he will flee from you.**"*

James 4:7

Day 25

Sanctification of The Spirit

> *"But we are bound to give thanks to God always for you, brethren beloved by The Lord, because **God from the beginning chose you for salvation through sanctification by The Spirit and belief in the truth.**"*
> **2 Thessalonians 2: 13**

The word *sanctify* means to be *set apart* by God for His purposes. We will consider this in three parts:

- Upon repentance and turning to Christ, we are initially *set apart* by God The Holy Spirit and transferred from the kingdom of darkness into God's Kingdom of light, known as The Spiritual new birth or being born again. It is a process we cannot do ourselves; it is a work only God can do as a result of believing in Him and receiving His free gift of Salvation in Christ. So, right from the start, we are saved by God's Grace alone and not of our works.

- After that, we are continually being set apart by The Holy Spirit throughout our lifetime in a collaborative process. We are delivered from the flesh, learning to walk in The Spirit and adhering to God's Word, which is achieved through our willingness to submit to God.

- Finally, when Christ comes again, or we die and go to be with The Lord, we are *set apart* by God from the very presence of sin. Only God can do this! So, we begin by His Grace and are ultimately saved by His Grace!

Firstly, the moment we believe in Jesus, God sets us apart from the kingdom of darkness and places us into His Kingdom of Light! A change of position occurs. Here we see a miraculous work of God in that He alone, without our involvement, separates us into His Kingdom, being born of The Holy Spirit. The Bible says we are made alive! We are translated from the kingdom of darkness into His marvellous Light! Spiritually speaking, this takes me to a different place! Yes, I am still residing in the presence of sin upon the earth, but Heaven has suddenly opened to me!

> "*He has delivered us from the **power of darkness and conveyed (translated) us into the kingdom of the Son of His love**, in whom we have redemption through His blood, the forgiveness of sins.*
>
> **Colossians 1:13**

*"...to open their eyes, to turn them from **darkness to light, and from the power of Satan to God**, that they may receive forgiveness of sins and an inheritance among **those who are sanctified by faith in Me.**"*

Acts 26: 17-18

Before we believed in The Lord, our spirit was dead to God, and we were fallen creatures destined for Hell, but now, having accepted Christ as our Saviour, we receive His life-giving Spirit and are suddenly made alive spiritually, being transferred into God's Kingdom! How did this happen?

Our position changed in its entirety because of faith in the shed Blood of Jesus Christ. You will find that everything about our Salvation through Jesus is because of this, and it is always a good thing to remind ourselves of just a few things Jesus has done for us!

- He forgives us;
- He has purchased us as His own possession;
- He cleanses us from sin and its power;
- He sanctifies us - or sets us apart to God - for His purposes; and especially,
- He loves us and gives us eternal life!

In other words, the moment we are drawn by The Spirit of God to Jesus and repent, thereby having our eyes opened, we receive eternal life and belong to God! This fact is so good we cannot rush past it! Let us re-iterate and amplify some points again!

In being set apart from the world, the believer is separated from The Spiritual dominion of the ruler of this world, Satan, and placed into The Spiritual realm of The Spirit and Christ's presence! Remember Jesus said to Pilate,

> **"My kingdom is not of this world.** *If My kingdom were of this world, My servants would fight, so that I should not be delivered to the Jews; but now **My kingdom is not from here.**"*
> **John 18:36**

The believer moves from the kingdom of darkness and joins Christ, becoming part of the Kingdom of God, which is of incredible significance! We become citizens of Heaven, children of God, and sit with Christ in the Heavenly Places! We belong to Him as His purchased possession, and all this takes place here and now and not when we die!

After this, Sanctification continues to the next important phase lasting a lifetime. God now sets us apart to change us from our old carnal life and way of thinking into His life and way of thinking! God thinks differently to you and me! He says,

> *"For My thoughts are not your thoughts,*
> *Nor are your ways My ways," says The Lord.*
> *"For as the heavens are higher than the earth,*
> *So are My ways higher than your ways,*
> *And My thoughts than your thoughts."*
> **Jeremiah 55:8-9**

So, it is not sufficient to God that we do our best or turn over a new leaf! God requires a new heart for man in likeness to that of His beloved Son. A heart that will love Him and which is no longer selfish, the former being the attributes of the new man and the latter that of the old. For this reason, He has gone to great lengths and paid such a great price on our behalf so that we could be forgiven and sanctified, a process that will continue until we go to be with The Lord. It is a fact that man's carnal nature and The Spirit are in opposition.

> *"For **the flesh lusts against The Spirit, and The Spirit against the flesh; and these are contrary to one another**, so that you do not do the things that you wish."*
> **Galatians 5:17**

Because man is born corrupted by sin and his nature is a slave to it, one of God's first things is to cleanse man's sinful heart. Only God can cleanse a person from the power of sin, and this cleansing or purifying is achieved only through the Blood of Jesus Christ. Therefore, having been set apart by God from the very beginning, He now prepares the way for our new life in Christ.

This stage is so important and vital for believers if we are to progress spiritually in accordance with God's individual plan for each of His children. We are called to submit to The Spirit and be led by Him to grow in Grace and the knowledge of The Lord. This crucial aspect of our sanctification will depend upon our willingness to follow The Lord and yield to Him! You see, we are part of the process! We must submit to The Lordship of Christ. The nitty-gritty is, our free will always be a part of the process because God wanted man to love and obey Him freely, which requires a choice - my choice!

The mission of The Holy Spirit is to fashion and change me from glory to glory to be like Christ. God desires that we should be conformed to the image of His Son!

> *"For whom He foreknew, He also predestined to be **conformed to the image of His Son.**"*
> **Romans 8:29**

God's High Calling for believers is, as we submit to Christ, we will not only be delivered from the guilt of sin, but be progressively washed from its pollution, saved from its power, and enabled, through Grace, to love and serve God. Never forget that Jesus made our sanctification possible through the offering of His shed blood on the cross. By accepting God's call, by The Spirit, to believe in His Son through repentance, we make a conscious decision to dedicate our souls, hearts, minds and bodies to God, a fact often omitted in modern-day evangelism but one God requires nevertheless!!

The following important and relevant passage of Scripture sums up our need for full allegiance to Christ.

> *"I beseech you therefore, brethren, by the mercies of God, that you present your bodies a living sacrifice, holy, acceptable to God, which is your reasonable service.* **And do not be conformed to this world, but be transformed by the renewing of your mind,** *that you may prove what is that good and acceptable and perfect will of God."*
>
> **Romans 12: 1-2**

Let us yield to the **HIGH CALLING OF GOD!**

This passage of Scripture at the beginning of Romans 12 forms a sound basis and summary for our Christian walk with God and tells us, primarily, of our requirement to submit ourselves to Him. A key factor highlighted here is the transformation of our mind's way of thinking to that of The Spirit's way of thinking. The more we come to God through His Word and prayer, abiding in the secret place, the more our thinking will change to that of The Spirit and not of the flesh. The Bible says we are given the ability to think completely differently through the mind of Christ, who dwells in us by The Spirit of God!

> *"... **put on The Lord Jesus Christ**, and make no provision for the flesh, to fulfil its lusts."*
>
> **Romans 13:14**

> *"For who has known the mind of The Lord that he may instruct Him?"* **But we have the mind of Christ.**
>
> **1 Corinthians 2:16**

So, you see, we can do this by co-operating with God. The power has been put within us! The Spirit of God is here! Therefore, each person must follow through on this commitment presenting their bodies as a living sacrifice to God. Whatever God asks us to do, remember, it will be achievable. Without this, there is no sanctification process, and we will remain carnal in our thinking with little or no spiritual development! If we are not developing spiritually, we cannot possibly do God's will, including those works God planned for us before we were born! We will fail to fully understand and appreciate God's full, abundant blessings that are ours in Christ! Therefore, let us put the interests and purposes of God's Kingdom first, making them our priority just as Jesus taught saying,

> *"But seek first the kingdom of God and His righteousness, and all these things shall be added to you."*
>
> **Matthew 6:33**

Let us be devoted to God! Let us yield ourselves to Him in humility! We have a new life in Christ; this is our privilege and identity; this is who we really are and why we were born! We will find fulfillment in life by accomplishing those good works God created for each of us to do! It will enable us to be fruitful for God! It will prepare us for Eternity. Jesus has promised to give a reward to each one according to their works at His coming! Will you live for Eternity with the God who loved you and gave Himself for you?

> *"And behold, I am coming quickly, and **My reward is with Me, to give to everyone according to his work."***
> **Revelation 22:12**

Finally, God sets apart each one of His children when all our service on earth is done. When we go to be with The Lord, the final process of Sanctification will take place, and God will *set us apart* from the **very presence of sin!** That is going to be very special! What a day that will be!

Part of a Famous Hymn:

What a Day That Will Be.

There is coming a day
When no heartaches shall come
No more clouds in the sky
No more tears to dim the eye
All is peace forever more
On that happy golden shore
What a day, glorious day that will be

What a day that will be
When my Jesus I shall see
When I look upon His face
The One who saved me by His grace
When He takes me by the hand
And leads me to the Promised Land
What a day, glorious day that will be
Lyrics and music by Jim Hill

"They will see his face, and his name will be on their foreheads."
Revelation 22:4

Thoughts for the Day

God says,
"I have even called you by your name;
I have named you, though you have not known Me.
I am The Lord, and there is no other;
There is no God besides Me.
I will gird you, though you have not known Me,"
Isaiah 45:4-5

"The crooked places shall be made straight
And the rough places smooth."
Isaiah 40:4b

PART 5

God's Eternal Laws

Day 26

Thinking Differently - Kingdom Laws

> *"...do not be conformed to this world, **but be transformed by the renewing of your mind**, that you may prove what is that good and acceptable and perfect will of God."*
> **Romans 12:2**

We have seen what our position is! As children of God, we are in the world but not of the world! Born again into God's Kingdom, the Bible says we have been transferred or translated from one Kingdom to another, that is, from the Kingdom of Darkness into His marvellous light! While we were under the power and control of the devil, who rules the Earthly Kingdoms by his principalities and evil powers, we were described as dead and spiritually inactive, but now, having been born into God's Kingdom, we have been made alive unto God!

> "And you **He made alive, who were dead** in trespasses and sins…"
>
> **Ephesians 2:1a**

As members of God's Kingdom and the Body of Christ, we need a new mindset, which is not readily understood, but it is impossible to live in God's Kingdom with an earthly perspective! Like oil and water, the two do not mix! Today's passage of Scripture calls us to think differently by no longer being conformed to this world but to be transformed by the renewing of our minds. The contrast intended here is between this world's ways of corruption compared to God's way of thinking found in God's pure Word. Much of this adjustment highlights the gulf and conflict between the flesh and The Spirit as outlined on Day 24 when we looked at *Sanctification of The Spirit.*

There are, however, other things we need to consider and learn from God's Word regarding Kingdom laws and the way Heaven operates, which will be new to us but most enlightening and welcome!
Given that we are now citizens of a new Kingdom, it follows that we should study The Scriptures to see for ourselves how that Kingdom operates.

The difficulty here is perhaps obvious, we may belong to another country called the Kingdom of God, but our physical life is here on Earth where we live, therefore our minds, by default, still tend to look earthwards, if only from time to time!

However, notwithstanding, we have responsibilities in this life to work for a living and perhaps raise a family. To The Spiritually zealous, it is a mistake to suppose, in the slightest way, that these earthly responsibilities are in themselves a hindrance from our service to The Lord as some have erroneously thought! There can be no excuse for being irresponsible to our earthly commitments under the pretext of serving God! According to God's way, raising a family is itself a Holy service since you are potentially bringing children into His Heavenly Kingdom and that for all Eternity!
We are sojourners upon Earth, and this world ultimately is not our real home; man's life does not consist of his earthy status and possessions.

> "And Jesus said to them, "Take heed and beware of covetousness, for **one's life does not consist in the abundance of the things he possesses."**
>
> **Luke 12:15**

Consequently, we must learn to look upwards and earthwards in a harmonious balance. We must learn the laws and principles of God through His written Word and apply them into our lives upon earth, effectively opening the miraculous dimension of God's Kingdom into our life. We will perform the responsibilities that are necessary with God's help and blessing. The challenge is this, are we willing to step out in faith to apply God's Word and put our faith and trust in His Kingdom laws? What sort of laws and principles are we talking about?

There are some Eternal truths in the Word of God which never change throughout time irrespective of what Covenant with God under which we may live. For example, the law of seedtime and harvest! Farmers respect and trust this Divine Law!

> *"While the earth remains,**Seedtime and harvest**,Cold and heat,Winter and summer,And day and night Shall not cease."*
> **Genesis 8:22**

At one time, some Farmers would apply the principle of *resting upon the Sabbath* to their farming methods! They would plant crops in a field for six consecutive years, and on the seventh year, they would leave it untouched to rest. Modern farming methods use fertilizers and organic manure to replenish the soil of its nutrients every year and, therefore, see no need to *rest the ground.*

One farmer planted his crop on land that had rested for a year, and he had a bumper crop far exceeding all other farmers around! There was a blight that year bringing disease, causing spoiled crops nationwide, but his field alone was untouched by it! God's laws always work, but will we trust them? Some would have argued that it was a waste of ground and money not to plant upon the field, but the outcome proved otherwise the following year! Those who honour and obey such Divine Laws and convictions by faith will prosper, but human reasoning can rob and stifle us of God's blessings. Through fear and unbelief, we can never enter the land of abundance and prosperity!

The principle of *seedtime and harvest* can be applied spiritually to other things in life, providing wisdom and understanding based upon God's Eternal laws!

> *"Do not be deceived, God is not mocked; for whatever a man **sows**, that he will also **reap**."*
> **Galatians 6:7**

This verse has a negative context, implying whoever sows evil in the sight of God will not go unpunished and ultimately will reap its consequences! These repercussions can still rise to the surface even if the person comes to know The Lord later! In such cases, all things must be brought to the light and dealt with through repentance, reconciliation, and especially forgiveness towards whomsoever may have been the injured party. God works in this way. Bringing things to light in humility and dealing with matters in God's way is the only path we can take to be free of any obstacles from the past. We glorify God when we confess our wrongdoings to others and openly express forgiveness even if they do not reciprocate or accept reconciliation. We will have done the right thing before a Holy, all-seeing God.

The Value of Diligence

The verse *"for whatever a man sows, that he will also reap"* can, in theory, also be applied in a positive situation. As well as sowing evil, one can equally sow good!

The *"sowing"* can be through putting in hard work for an examination or yielding one's life towards a good cause or perhaps putting work, effort, and sacrifice into a business. One day the person will reap the benefits if they have acted with integrity! That's the way it is! It's an Eternal law for all!

The application does not have to be figurative, for if a gardener prepares the soil with compost and other soil nutrients before planting his seed and if he meticulously cares for the plants as they grow, he can expect a good crop and will reap what he has sown!
A friend of mine specialises in growing prize roses. He feeds them with bonemeal about every four to five weeks during the growing months, amongst other things. People ask him just how he can grow such beautiful large rose blooms! *What you put in, you get out* to use a modern rendering of this Scripture!
Finally, for today, we will look at one more Divine Law though there are so many in God's Word!

> *"Cast your bread upon the waters, for you will find it after many days."*
> **Ecclesiastes 11:1**

In its context, and in line with the rest of Scripture, this verse has to do with being generous, and someday you will be rewarded. Some would say, *Do good wherever you go, and after a while, the good you do will come back to you.* Literally speaking, casting bread on water seems to be a pointless exercise! Similarly, there are many things in life that may appear to be a waste of time and effort, but the truth is you do not know what the results will yield!

> *"The one who **sows righteousness** reaps a sure reward."*
> **Proverbs 11: 18**

> *"Let us not become weary in doing good, for at the proper time we will **reap a harvest** if we do not give up (lose heart.)"*
> **Galatians 6:9**

There was an occasion in my life when the Scripture **Ecclesiastes 11:1** vividly came to mind. It goes back many years to when I was in my thirties and living in London.

There was a particular chapter of my life when I taught Sunday School in South Acton,[1,] together with three others teachers. It was no ordinary Sunday School! Our church S.S. was taking place elsewhere while we were involved in reaching out to children in the highways and byways - in the open air! During the winter months, we used an old hut so we could carry on the work. The children did not have parents in the church and knew nothing of discipline and how to behave! Therefore, every meeting was always going to be very challenging, and the children could be most unruly, but we persevered for several years! When I arrived home in the late afternoon, I often felt quite exhausted and quickly fell asleep for an hour before attending the evening service at our Church!

Some four or five years later, we had left the church in Acton and were attending an Elim Pentecostal church at Northfields situated furthermore west of Acton as you travel out of London. I had qualified to be an elder in that church, having spent five or more years at another Elim church at Notting Hill Gate, where we had got married. There were strict requirements in becoming an elder, and the pastor desired me to take up office in those days. After contacting my previous pastor to verify my attendance at his church and an affirmative vote by the congregation, I was duly appointed.

    The purpose of explaining this background was this: As an elder, I could be chosen to do certain duties by the pastor, such as preaching. On occasions, I went into the water baptism tank to assist the pastor in baptising people. It was upon such an occasion at a water baptism service that a great surprise awaited me! Each baptismal candidate would come along and give their testimony about how they had become a Christian. They would be immersed in the water and brought up signifying that they had died to the old way of life and had now risen to newness of life in Christ, in obedience to Scripture. They promised to serve and follow their Lord and Saviour, Jesus Christ.

    After being baptised, the ladies would go to one changing room on the left, and the men would go to another room on the right. When all was finished, I went to the men's changing room to get changed. There was a young man there, who after a while, spoke to me with words to the effect, *"I remember you, sir!"*

I turned and looked intensely at him as he stood smiling at me, then asked him where I had seen him before. He replied, *"It was in your Sunday School in South Acton!"*

The memory of a certain cheeky young lad came before me! *"So, it was!"* I replied with amazement! *"So, it was!"* As I mused over that event, The Lord brought the following Scripture to mind in the evening quietness.

> *"Cast your bread upon the waters, for you will find it after many days."*

If working in that Sunday School in South Acton brought about this one miracle of change, it would have been worth it all for God's Kingdom!

Sometimes we must sacrifice, in seemingly impossible, futile situations, our time and effort persevering for the sake of The Gospel; we have to give out God's Word, the Bread of Life, to the "whosoever," and God says that it will not return to Him void!

Prayer

> *Fill me, O Lord, with Your Wisdom and understanding that I may apply my heart to the knowledge of God.*

Show and direct me according to Your Word;
Show me the path that leads to life - Your life for me.

> *The world sounds many voices, and they change like the wind, but Your Word endures and never changes!*

*Teach me continuously so that I do not wander astray from Your Law.
Your Word alone is reliable and to be trusted.
Blessed be the Name of The Lord!*

Day 27

God's Conditional Promises

Over time, as we read and study God's Word in both the Old and New Testaments, we find that God makes some conditional promises. They are usually introduced by the words *"If…* and end with…*then"* For example:

> *"**If** My people who are called by My name will humble themselves, and pray and seek My face, and turn from their wicked ways, **then** I will hear from heaven, and will forgive their sin and heal their land."*
> **2 Chronicles 7:14**

Such conditional promises of God are especially worth our attention. Think of it. God says one thing: if we receive it into our hearts and act upon it, He promises a specific outcome! This challenges us because, by its very nature, it is not so much a commandment but an invitation; it's as if we have a choice; it is an open door for us to choose to enter or not! It is *outside the box* for the *status quo* child of God who thus far has only done the things expected and not accustomed to venturing out too far into the *depths of God's waters*.

Sometimes, God seeks to draw apart those who sincerely desire Him above everything else; those who want a more intimate relationship with Him; those who desire everything God has for them? Look at the challenge and directness in the following open-ended verse:

> *"And you will seek Me and find Me, when you **search for Me with all your heart**."*
> **Jeremiah 29:13**

What does it mean to *seek God with all your heart*? What makes this different from seeking God? Some might suggest that *this is not quantifiable with a certain amount of time or effort, so how do I know when I have accomplished this?* Yet, most will understand something of what God means here! They are to seek Him earnestly and honestly, and since the heart is specified to be involved, we are to come openly confessing our utter need before God in total surrender. Scripture suggests the need to come in closer to find God, getting to know Him through His Word just as if the person had wandered astray and is now being called back! God calls such people to return to Him.

> *"Let the wicked forsake his way,*
> *And the unrighteous man his thoughts;*
> ***Let him return to The Lord,***
> ***And He will have mercy on him;***
> ***And to our God,***
> ***For He will abundantly pardon."***
>
> **Isaiah 55:7**

So often, we can end up settling for a ritual routine allocating a time to pray and a time to read God's Word, yet the implication here implies going above and beyond this! It is not the habitual practice called into question but rather the intensity or degree of earnestness!

The following is a conditional passage with significant implications for someone who has this frame of mind and heart.

> *"My son, **if** you receive my words, and (**if you**) treasure my commands within you, so that you incline your ear to wisdom, and apply your heart to understanding; Yes, **if** you cry out for discernment, and (**if you**) lift up your voice for understanding, **if** you seek her as silver, and search for her as for hidden treasures; **then** you will understand the fear of The Lord, and find the knowledge of God."*
>
> **Proverbs 2:1-5**

One Sunday morning at church, we had a guest speaker. He spoke about *"Seek the Giver, not just the Gift!"* His words challenged me the moment I heard them. He followed on by saying, *"What is greater, the **gift** or the **giver** of the gift?"*

Obviously, the giver of the gift is the greater! The Bible is full of examples where God requires us to ask of Him to receive and be full, yet this was different. The speaker did not say to ask God for anything, only to seek the Giver more! I thought, *"When was the last time I prayed to God without asking Him for the usual requests but instead sought Him for Who He is and not just for what I or someone else could receive!?"*

This became a turning point in my spiritual life and relationship with God. I had been a Christian for more than forty years, involved with much service within the church. I had held office as a Sunday School Superintendent, deacon and elder, yet I needed something more! God was calling me to come closer to Him.! He did not desire me to do more "service" or have some special "calling" to do a work but rather to seek Him alone.

I left the service quite excited, facing a new venture! That evening, I picked up my Bible and went into a quiet room, closing the door behind me. After reading the Psalms for a time, I placed my Bible down and got on my knees to pray. I thought of the Scripture in **Psalm 46:10** that says, *"Be still and know that I am God."* I began to thank God for Jesus, for saving me a sinner and for His Word. I continued in that manner for a long while. It was good! I felt the presence of The Spirit. I recalled that the psalmist spoke much about receiving God's attributes for himself, things that I have never heard people pray for, so I began to pray in the same way,

> *"Teach me Your Word; Fill me with Your love; Show me Your paths that I might walk in them;Teach me Your ways; I desire to be like You."*

By praying in this more intimate, open, and personal fashion regularly, it became clear over time that God was changing me in ways I had not particularly asked for or even thought about, but God changed me anyway! It was as though God was downloading into my heart His nature and qualities, things that a person could never imitate or achieve by themselves. For example, while God hates our sin, He loves the sinner. He loves people, and my love increased so that I see every person as special. As a result, I found it easier to talk to people and share my testimony and the wonderful news of The Gospel. Compassion increased, as did my faith and trust in the Living God. I became less afraid and anxious about the many problems that face everyone in the world and daily life. In short, God was much more real and personal to me, and I began serving Him in a new and different way!

MEDITATION

Paul, the Apostle, once said,

> "...that I may know Him and the power of His resurrection...."
>
> **Philippians 3:10**

Day 28

Will A Man Rob God?

> *"' Will a man rob God? Yet you have robbed Me!'*
> *But you say, 'In what way have we robbed You?'*
> ***'In tithes and offerings.'"***
>
> **Malachi 3:8**

In the above passage of Scripture, we read how God's people had forsaken the giving of tithes, and consequently, the House of God had no produce so that the priesthood could not function!

Under the Law, tithing was a requirement instituted by God. From a practical point of view, this was essential to provide sustenance for the Priesthood because God required them to work continuously in the Temple, and they could not work and earn wages like the rest of God's people. God appointed the tribe of Levi to perform these duties, and no one else was allowed to do so.

It follows that this particular tribe were dependent upon the tithes of the people for their finances and well-being.

It is important to realize that God had ordained this system for the Levites' welfare through the tithes of the people; therefore, by tithing, they enabled God's purposes to be accomplished but, as this passage indicates, without them, His purposes could not be fulfilled.

We can easily fail to understand this principle today, seemingly being oblivious that God requires our giving to operate. God has ordained this principle, that is, one of mutual co-operation of giving to Him. Although the tithe belongs to God, yet He requires our willingness to bring it to His storehouse, which is that part of the church or assembly of God's people, where we serve Him. According to the above passage of Scripture, God deliberately and purposefully places this requirement upon His people to provide tithes or one-tenth in His storehouse funds. Reference to the New Testament will reveal how that the Apostles required offerings to be made for the work of God's Kingdom. God requires our commitment in all our service to Him, particularly providing for His Body, the Church which he has purchased with His blood, and, importantly, in extending His Kingdom.

It is interesting to see how God declared His people were robbing Him by not giving their tithe! He implies that one-tenth belongs to Him. If you steal from someone, you take for yourself what is theirs, or as in this case, hold back that which belongs to them! However, there is a much deeper concept to be addressed. It involves a personal covenant relationship of faith in God and His conditional promise of abundant provision for those who will trust Him with all of their finances. It is a covenant that spans both the New and Old Testaments and is outside of any Law.

Jesus did not abolish the tithe in the New Testament but made us more aware that **everything belongs to Him** and that we are only stewards and trustees of all that he has given to us. Money, houses and possessions all belong to God!

He taught us to give, not hoard! For example, if you have two coats, give one away to someone in need. The following Scripture gives us a general principle for giving to those in need when it is in our power to do so!

*"**Do not withhold** good from those to whom it is due, when it is in the power of your hand to do so."*

Proverbs 3:27

I have been called upon many times to obey this command upon seeing others in need. All belongs to God. He gives to us so that we can provide for others. As it is written,

"Freely you have received, freely give."
Matthew 10:8

Practical Kingdom living is unselfish; it is giving bountifully and not holding back! God calls us to no longer live earthly lives, but Kingdom Lives with Christ as our chief example! Remember that well-quoted Scripture, *"Jesus is the Way, the Truth and the Life?"* We need to apply it in every practical aspect of our life!
Jesus has shown us what true giving is! As *Isaac Watts* wrote in that famous Hymn published in 1707:

> *Were the whole realm of nature mine,*
> *That were an offering far too small;*
> *Love so amazing, so divine,*
> **Demands my soul, my life, my all.**

When he wrote this hymn, Isaac Watts realised that *giving* to God is immeasurable. Yet, some would wrestle with financial giving, especially tithing, which merely specifies a set amount to give! Alarmingly, the whole idea of *not giving financially* into a church is increasingly common, and that of tithing hardly exists and is foreign to many people and churches! Their pretext is that God will provide! Ask yourself this question, **"How did God provide for the welfare of the tribe of Levi?"**
Then ask yourself, **"Will God provide for that which He has called me to provide?**

The whole ethos of the Bible is to live for God, seeking first His Kingdom, sacrificing all to follow Him, and yet this is hardly reflected when it comes to this matter of giving to God what lies in our pockets! What is lacking here is a spiritual understanding of Kingdom living! We are merely custodians of the blessings God has bestowed upon us. What do we possess that we have not received?

In the middle ages, the people in the land took this passage of Scripture very seriously. In obedience to God's Word, they built storehouses called *Tithe Barns*, where all the farmers brought one-tenth of all their produce to God's storehouse, the Church, for distribution. It is worthy to note that there was much poverty across the land with few amenities or modern appliances, yet these people tithed and were blessed! They understood this in the seventeenth century, so how far have we progressed in the church spiritually in the twenty-first century?

Some would point to the fact that tithing is in the Old Testament Law, and today we are not under The Law! Well, this statement is not true! Tithing, in principle, is not unique to the Law of Moses but existed from the very beginning! In fact, Tithing existed as far back as Abraham!

An occasion occurred when Abraham had just won a battle taking all its spoils. Suddenly, Melchizedek, Priest and King of Salem turned up on the scene bearing gifts of bread and wine to give to Abraham. However, Abraham gave Melchizedek a tenth of all his spoils of war! He recognised Melchizedek as a representative of the God whom he worshiped, and he paid homage to Him. In this respect, Abraham's tithe was both an offering and an act of worship to God. Tithing, therefore, in essence, is an act of worship and reverence to Almighty God.

Now, there was no legal requirement for Abraham to give a tithe since the Laws of Moses did not exist then! Therefore, the people's obligation to give a tithe to the tribe of Levi did not apply here! Abraham gave a tithe outside of the Law! Consequently, it is entirely erroneous to think of tithing as an aspect of the Law that no longer applies today since Tithing was done outside the Law by Abraham!

What exactly does the New Testament say about giving? We will be ashamed, for, in the early church, they literally sold land and brought everything to the Apostles' feet!

> "...all who were possessors of lands or houses sold them and brought the proceeds of the things that were sold, and laid them at the apostles' feet, and they distributed to each as anyone had need."
> **Acts 4: 34-35**

What an act of love and commitment to the work of God! Furthermoremore, gifts for God's work were expected.

> "But this I say: **He who sows sparingly will also reap sparingly, and he who sows bountifully will also reap bountifully.** So, let each one give as he purposes in his heart, not grudgingly or of necessity; for God loves a cheerful giver."
> **2 Corinthians 9:6-7**

The Apostle refers to that eternal, unchanging law of seedtime and harvest and uses this as a yardstick!

Jesus spoke in a similar fashion, comparing the act of giving with planting a seed to obtain a harvest stating that with the same measure that you use, it will be measured back to you."

> *"Give, and it will be given to you: good measure, pressed down, shaken together, and running over will be put into your bosom. For **with the same measure that you use, it will be measured back to you.**"*
> **Luke 6:8**

The context of this passage of Scripture is that of filling a sack with seed. To maximise the quantity of grain, you shake the sack, press it down then shake it again until the grain seed runs over! God uses this measure to bless those who give generously!
Reference to the kind of giving associated within Christ's teaching in the New Testament, if anything, **places tithing as God's minimum standard**! Jesus did not specifically talk about tithing. Why? Because He raised the bar from one-tenth to **giving Him our all**! In fact, every good thing we are, have and own is received from His good hand! Jesus made us more aware that everything belongs to Him and that we are only stewards and trustees.
Jesus saw that money and possessions were a problem and, in fact, were a selfish stronghold right at the heart of sinful human nature. He spoke of the futility of trusting in riches, saying that,

"The love of money is the root of all evil! What shall it profit a man if he gain the whole world but loses his own soul? A man's life does not consist of the abundance of the things he possesses!

When a rich young ruler came to Jesus asking what he should do to obtain eternal life, Jesus told him to go and sell all he had and follow Him, and great would be his reward in Heaven. This Jesus said to point out how much we are ruled in our old human nature by money. He revealed the sort of mindset we can have focused upon this world alone and not upon Eternity!
For this reason, it is not only good to give but also to allow God to have supremacy over all we have and do. By giving constructively, we are de-throning the power that money has over us, and in so doing, we become free to follow a generous and giving God! Make no mistake, unless we learn to give generously in love and in proportion to what we have, we shall limit how far we can enter a deep and personal relationship with God! True, God wants our hearts and not so much our money, but the only way to achieve such is by testing our willingness to surrender to Him those things that hinder us. Such teachings are far higher than the Law ever could be! Jesus searches the heart and its motive - something the Law could never do!

As we have seen, tithing existed before the Law of Moses. Therefore, it can be considered as having no fundamental association with it but rather everything to do with the same kind of worship and respect shown by Abraham towards God. What exactly is God saying in the following passage?

> *"Will a man rob God? Yet you have robbed Me! But you say, 'In what way have we robbed You?' 'In tithes and offerings. You are cursed with a curse, For you have robbed Me, Even this whole nation.* **Bring all the tithes into the storehouse, that there may be food in My house, and try Me now in this,"** *Says The Lord of hosts,* **"If I will not open for you the windows of heaven And pour out for you such blessing That there will not be room enough to receive it."**
>
> Malachi 3: 8-10

"Try Me now in this," Says The Lord of hosts!

Firstly, God has said that the tithe belongs to Him, and through it, He will establish a covenant relationship with those who will bring it into His storehouse! It is the key that unlocks a spiritual door between God and man! Let us look at the second part of the Scripture:

> *"Bring all the tithes into the storehouse, That there may be food in My house,* ***And try Me now in this,"*** *Says The Lord of hosts, "If I will not open for you the windows of heaven And pour out for you such blessing That there will not be room enough to receive it."*

God does the unprecedented! He asks us to *try Him* in this! The promise is conditional, but the blessings to follow are certain since God declares it with His title and Name - ***The Lord of hosts***!

Know this, that God will not only provide, as He implies when He says,

> *"If I will not open for you the windows of Heaven and pour out for you such blessing that there will not be room enough to receive it."*

He will also work to protect all your finances showing you what wise and unwise spending is! You will be allowing God to do this! Your money is now His money but is on loan to you, so be sure God will be a good manager of it but remember, He will need your will and co-operation in everything! He will personally be committed to every aspect of your life that involves money! As you ask God for help, guidance, and protection, He will hear you! He will protect you in practical ways to not fall victim to unscrupulous people who might seek to over-charge and rob you.

This is the beginning of the blessing He promises to bestow upon you! God says He will pour them out over you! It speaks of an overflow of blessing so that you can give and then give again, continually bringing glory to His Name. Over time, the world will notice that you are prosperous; that is, God is touching your whole life and well-being! The church will prosper with no lack and will itself be able to give a tithe of all offerings to the poor and needy! Outsiders will see that your God does indeed bless and make you generous!

What picture do they see right now?

God has always desired a full, whole-hearted relationship, and He establishes any aspect of His relationship with man through a Covenant.

Every born-again child of God benefits from the Covenant in the blood of Jesus. In this Covenant, we are completely forgiven and translated into God's Kingdom as the purchased possession of Christ. *We are not our own*! The Bible says, *"We are bought with a price!"*

> *"Or do you not know that your body is the temple of The Holy Spirit who is in you, whom you have from God, and you are not your own? For you were bought at a price; therefore, glorify God in your body and in your spirit, which are God's."*
> **1 Corinthians 6:19-20**

Whilst we are all familiar with the *"forgiven"* aspect of our Salvation, the rest of this passage is not so pervasive! We can fail to realise or accept that God calls us to no longer live unto ourselves but unto Him. To know that we are totally secure in Him, having an eternal hope, is more precious than to own the wealth and riches of the whole world which are passing away! It shows us we are no longer on our own but that God has the highest regard for our lives and well-being!
I would rather be safe in the hands of the Eternal God who loves me than to live independently and selfishly, indulging miserably in the pleasures of sin for a season!

Only as the details unfold from the Word of God and become written upon our hearts do we fully realise our position in Christ. As incredible as this is, the reality is not always clear to many. Our vision can quickly become blurred by the *here and now,* for we are living in the world with its fears, uncertainties, pressures, temptations and lusts! Faith is required to embrace this reality of who we are in Christ, thus enabling us to live under His Lordship and Kingdom rule! We can do it if we choose to stay strong and unwavering in faith.!
Whether in the Old or New Testaments of Scripture, the choice for God's people to live for themselves and their own desires or by faith, to live by God's Word has always been the stumbling block! God's people of old did not want this!

On one occasion, the people came to Samuel asking that he give them a king to rule over them to be like all the other nations! It displeased God, and when Samuel inquired of Him, He told him not to feel despondent, for they had not rejected him, but they had rejected God from ruling over them!
Walking with God will always benefit our faith and confidence, and this morning's topic is no exception. Let us seek to prove God by taking Him at His Word! After all, that is what we are required to do as His children - is it not?

Meditation

"God is not a man, that He should lie, Nor a son of man, that He should repent.
Has He said, and will He not do? Or has He spoken, and will He not make it good?"
Numbers 23:19

PART 6

Seated with Christ

Day 29

There is Power in the Name of Jesus

> *"And being found in appearance as a man,* **He humbled Himself** *and became obedient to the point of death, even the death of the cross. Therefore,* **God also has highly exalted Him and given Him the name which is above every name,** *that at the name of Jesus every knee should bow..."*
>
> **Philippians 2: 8 -10**

Today we will look at why the Name of Jesus is so powerful! So much so, in fact, that there is no other name whether in Heaven, on Earth or under the earth that is higher, above, or more important!

We know that Jesus has conquered the power of death, and this includes all the principalities and powers of darkness, but did you know that when regenerate man puts his faith in that Name, there is power unleashed to rebuke and bring down these powers of darkness? God has given this authority to us, His Church which is the Body of Christ!

The early disciples were familiar with the many miracles performed by Jesus. After His resurrection, Jesus called His disciples together and gave them power and authority over all demons, and to cure diseases. He sent them into all the world to preach The Gospel and to heal the sick. After the day of Pentecost, when The Holy Spirit was poured out upon them, the disciples received boldness to preach, teach and pray for the sick just as Jesus had promised! The following was one such time.

> *"Now Peter and John went up together to the temple at the hour of prayer, the ninth hour. And a certain man lame from his mother's womb was carried, whom they laid daily at the gate of the temple which is called Beautiful, to ask alms from those who entered the temple… Then* **Peter said,** *"Silver and gold I do not have, but what I do have I give you:* **In the name of Jesus Christ of Nazareth, rise up and walk"**
>
> **Acts 3: 1-2, 6**

Peter stated an important fact to the people! The lame man was healed, not by the physical presence of Jesus because He was in heaven, but **through faith in the Name of Jesus!** Now, clearly, the disciples had no power of themselves to heal the man. However, they did have the presence and power of The Holy Spirit, who endorsed and confirmed their faith *in the Name of Jesus* by healing and raising the man from his bed of infirmity!

> *"Men of Israel, why do you marvel at this? Or why look so intently at us, **as though by our own power or godliness we had made this man walk?"*** **(v12)**

According to the faith displayed in that Name, the name above all names, The Spirit of God responded. Notice three things happening.

- The disciples had faith in the Name of Jesus.
- Peter stepped out in faith and spoke the *Word of God* with authority.
- The Holy Spirit confirmed it and healed the lame man.

To understand why there is power in the Name of Jesus, we need to look at the Person who owns that Name, and this we will do by focusing upon today's opening passage of Scripture broken into three parts:

Part 1

"Jesus made Himself of no reputation, (emptied Himself) taking the form of a bondservant, and coming in the likeness of men." **(verse 7)**

Firstly, the Scripture tells us He made Himself of no reputation; Jesus *emptied Himself* of all His privileges - though not of His deity. In other words, He was still the eternal God but made as a man subjecting Himself to that of a bondservant. Jesus veiled His deity and took upon Himself real humanity!

As a man, Jesus became a ***bondservant***, which literally means ***to bind*** (Greek – *Doulos*) or be in bondage or subjection to another - for example, as a slave. Jesus came into this world assuming no special rights or privileges, not even those of a natural servant. Rather, He subjected Himself entirely to serving God His Father with utter, unreserved obedience!

The verse also states that Jesus came *in the likeness of men*. Jesus had the outward form of humanity, and this form - this true humanity - was added to His deity. In other words, Jesus was indeed a man but, He was more than that. His being was still Divine!

As the Christmas Hymn says,

> *Veiled in flesh the Godhead see,*
> *Hail the incarnate Deity!*
> *Pleased as man with man to dwell,*
> *Jesus our Immanuel.*

"Hark! the herald angels sing"
Charles Wesley (1707-1788)

Part 2

***"And being found in appearance as a man, He humbled Himself and became obedient to the point of death, even the death of the cross."* (Verse 8)**

Secondly, Jesus, God's eternal Son, was now wholly given to living the life of a man, a slave without exercising His own will but succumbing to The Father's will! Trying to imagine what this really entailed needs much consideration and thought! The first necessary quality was that of humility. God is humble! The Bible says of God,

*"I dwell in the high and holy place,**With him who has a contrite and humble spirit,**To revive The Spirit of the humble,And to revive the heart of the contrite ones."*

Isaiah 57:15

As He obeyed The Father, His life exhibited this quality of humility by coming down to the Earth in the first place! With every challenge facing Him, Jesus knew His way was to follow The Father's will, which meant learning obedience as a man! There were times when Jesus knew difficulties and suffering were coming His way, which would be challenging for any person to experience. Jesus cried out in the garden,

> *"Father, if it is Your will, take this cup away from Me; nevertheless, **not My will, but Yours, be done."** Then, an angel appeared to Him from heaven, strengthening Him. And being in agony, He prayed more earnestly. Then His sweat became like great drops of blood falling to the ground."*
> **Luke 22: 42-44**

The Bible teaches that Jesus *learned obedience by the things which He suffered!* As the Son of God, He chose to do the will of The Father in Eternity, but upon Earth, he had to do it for real!

> *"...who, in the days of His flesh, when He had offered up prayers and supplications, with vehement cries and tears to Him who was able to save Him from death, and was heard because of His godly fear,* ***though He was a Son, yet He learned obedience by the things which He suffered."***
> **Hebrews 5:7**

We cannot imagine the suffering and sacrifice of Jesus as He surrendered His will to The Father and experienced inflicted pain from sinful man! He became *the pure innocent spotless Lamb of God led as a lamb to the slaughter.* This was new to Him! The Psalmist prophesied saying,

> "You know my reproach, my shame, and my dishonour; My adversaries are all before You. **Reproach has broken my heart,** And I am full of heaviness; I looked for someone to take pity, but there was none; And for comforters, but I found none. **They also gave me gall for my food, And for my thirst they gave me vinegar to drink."**
> **Psalm 69: 19-21**

God was leading His Son along the way He needed to go, the way it was written of Him beforehand! Jesus knew all things in Heaven of how He would suffer, but now, it was all being made very clear and real in the flesh! The Bible says that **He** (The Father) **has put Him to grief!**

> "Because He had done no violence, Nor was any deceit in His mouth.
> Yet it pleased The Lord to bruise Him; He has put Him to grief."
> **Isaiah 53: 9-10**

There must have been an indescribable personal dilemma in the Godhead because The Father was directing His Son to experience those sufferings that were written of Him. He had to endure things in the flesh, things he had agreed to do in Eternity but yet needed to be fulfilled! We cannot begin to imagine the cost to God throughout the life of Jesus Christ His Son, *a man of sorrows and acquainted with grief* culminating in His death on a cross! Yes, we are the beneficiaries of a so-called, *free Salvation* but it was not free! Jesus obeyed The Father, and in so doing, He went to the cross; *He set His face like a flint* towards Jerusalem and would not relent! The Bible tells us that, in this sense, God The Father put Him to grief so that Jesus cried out to God, saying,

> *"My God, My God, why have You forsaken Me?"*

God had cut Him off, and Jesus felt it!

Part 3

> *"Therefore, God also has highly exalted Him and given Him the name which is above every name, that at the name of Jesus every knee should bow, of those in heaven, and of those on earth, and of those under the earth, and that every tongue should confess that Jesus Christ is Lord, to the glory of God The Father."*

Now we can understand much more about why there is power in the Name of Jesus! This final section begins with the word *"therefore"*, implying that all that has been said before has reached a conclusion. Therefore, what follows is highly significant, and we do well to read, memorise, and meditate upon it carefully! Why? God declares His approval of His Son by giving Him a Name higher than any other!

Reading the Scriptures in parts 1-2 a second time will help us focus upon the person of Jesus, namely His attitude of submission to The Father; His humility and obedience, which outlined what He did and reveals its exemplary nature regarding the way He did it! In The Father's eyes, His Son is the ultimate fulfilment of a perfect life exceeding all others. Therefore, God has exalted Him! This is why God has highly exalted Him and given Him the name *above every name!*

Earlier, it was stated, *"To understand why there is power in the Name of Jesus, we need to look at the Person who owns that Name;"*

Now we can see why! God accepted the sacrifice Jesus made through His obedience, and as a consequence, He has exalted Jesus far above all!

> *Far above all,*
> *Far above all*
> *God has exalted Him*
> *Far above all;*
> *Crown Him as Lord –*
> *at His feet humbly fall*
> *Jesus, Christ Jesus*
> *Is far above all*
>
> Redemption Hymnal 194

All God's children need to firmly take hold of this fact and believe that our power and authority originate from trusting in that Name. It is the only name God has exalted! It is God's perspective we adhere to and not our own!

It is new to us. The kind of obedience demonstrated by Jesus to His Father was to completely empty of self and be totally submissive! He is the blueprint of a life that pleases God, and we who say we abide in Him must all learn to walk as He walked! It is more to do with our commitment and loyalty than the ability to do so.

When God requires our obedience, it is necessary to do things in the way that please Him, wholeheartedly and with love and devotion ultimately fearing to disobey Him! God's Way is far above our way! Every step Jesus took had to glorify God to perfection - and it did!

We read an example of how not to obey God when the Children of Israel were in the wilderness. God was displeased with Moses when he struck the rock, in anger, with his rod instead of speaking to it to obtain water!

> *"Take the rod; you and your brother Aaron gather the congregation together.* **Speak to the rock before their eyes, and it will yield its water**...
> ...*Moses said to them, "Hear now you rebels! Must we bring water for you out of this rock?" Then* **Moses lifted his hand and struck the rock twice with his rod;** *and water came out abundantly*

> *...Then The Lord spoke to Moses and Aaron,* **"Because you did not believe Me, to hallow Me in the eyes of the children of Israel,** *therefore you shall not bring this assembly into the land which I have given them."*
> **Numbers 20: 8, 10-11, 12**

The children of Israel displayed exceedingly confrontational behaviour towards Moses and moaned continuously for water in the wilderness! Their attitude provoked Moses and Aaron into being impatient, frustrated, and angry! It was not the first time the people's discontent had provoked them, but it was the *last straw*! In doing so, they brought disrespect to **God's Name** by not hallowing it before the eyes of the people! God would provide the people with water, but **this was not the way to do it!** The reaction from Moses and Aaron dis-honoured God's Person in the eyes of the people. As God's chosen leaders, they stood before them, representing Him!

What we are seeing is that Jesus always brought honour and glory to His Father's Name before the people of His day! He obeyed God to the very letter whether it pleased the people or not!

This is what is meant by the perfect and obedient Son of Man; *the Faithful Witness*, who came and fulfilled all that was written of Him and executed it in the way God desired.

Jesus, unlike Moses, was *tempted in all points as we are yet without sin!* Only Jesus Christ has ever lived this kind of life of total obedience to perfection, that is by love alone with a perfect heart of submission honouring and bringing Glory to God! So, we praise the Name of Jesus, the Son of God who alone provides for God's mercy upon all who come to God through Him!

We read examples in The Word and observe just how Jesus reacted to men who belittled Him, abused Him, and ultimately crucified Him. Isaiah, by The Holy Spirit, foresaw these things and openly spoke when He said,

"He was oppressed and He was afflicted, **Yet He opened not His mouth;** *He was led as a lamb to the slaughter, And as a sheep before its shearers is silent,* **so, He opened not His mouth.** *"*
Isaiah 53: 7

The occasion below speaks of Jesus as He stood before Pilate and the Chief Priests just before His crucifixion.

"And while He was being accused by the chief priests and elders, ***He answered nothing…***
Then Pilate said to Him, ***"Do You not hear how many things they testify against You?"*** *But* ***He answered him not one word, so that the governor marvelled greatly."***
Matthew 27: 12-13

We can never be entirely like Jesus, but The Holy Spirit can reveal to us His Person, and in so doing, we must bow the knee before Him in total surrender worshipping Him as Lord and Saviour! There is no one else like Jesus, who was both God and man!
The Hymn writer said:

Were the whole realm of nature mine,
That were an offering far too small;
Love so amazing, so Divine,
Demands my soul, my life, my all.

"When I Survey the Wondrous Cross"
Isaac Watts - pub.1707

Meditation

Our confession of JESUS as LORD will invite His Presence and POWER over all evil, we face today!
As we declare His Lordship by faith, His rule enters our settings and circumstances!
This exalting and honour of Jesus is the hallmark of all POWER through FAITH in Him and His NAME!

THERE IS POWER IN THE NAME OF JESUS!

There is power in the name of Jesus
There is power in the name of Jesus
There is power in the name of Jesus
To break every chain, break every chain, break every chain

To break every chain, break every chain, break every chain
Gospel singer Tasha Cobbs
Born: 7 July 1981, Georgia, United States.

Day 30

Confessing the Name of Jesus

We should never imagine or suppose that speaking the Name of Jesus is a magic formula! We know only too well how the Name of Jesus is expressed in blasphemy and a derogatory manner.

There was an occasion of interest in the life of Paul when certain people attempted to imitate Him and cast out evil spirits! They had a surprise awaiting them!

> *"Then some of the itinerant Jewish exorcists took it upon themselves to call the name of The Lord Jesus over those who had evil spirits, saying,*
> *"We exorcise you by the Jesus whom Paul preaches." Also, there were seven sons of Sceva, a Jewish chief priest, who did so. And the evil spirit answered and said, "Jesus I know, and Paul I know; but who are you?"*
> *Then the man in whom the evil spirit was leaped on them, overpowered them, and prevailed against them, so that they fled out of that house naked and wounded."*
>
> **Acts 19:13-16**

Those who would exercise authority in the name of Jesus over evil spirits, principalities and powers in the Heavenly Places must themselves be regenerated by The Holy Spirit, that is, be born-again believers who know The Lord personally!

There is power and authority in the Name of Jesus, and yesterday we saw in detail why this is so! We saw what God was looking for and that He was satisfied with His Son and the finished work of the cross!

As ambassadors of Christ, we are called to demonstrate a good confession of faith, testifying to God's Grace and Mercy through our Lord Jesus Christ to a lost world. Yet many long-standing believers saved by His marvellous Grace fail, for whatever reason, to exhibit the Divine authority and conviction that comes with a true confession of their faith.

"...for with the heart one believes unto righteousness, and with the mouth confession is made unto salvation..."
Romans 10:10

If we never confess with our mouth The Lord Jesus Christ, which is a fundamental teaching of Scripture, our lives will be spiritually unfulfilled and incomplete. Believing and confessing are both required if we are to receive and confirm our salvation! Power is in the confessing - confessing the Name above every name, which brings glory to God!

"But be doers of the word, and not hearers only, deceiving yourselves."
James 1:22

Being a doer of the Word in this context is believing the Word and receiving it into your life, seeking to apply it! Then, and only then, will changes follow! Remember, it only is as we speak forth God's Word and confess our faith in Him that we defeat the enemy of our souls! In so doing, we establish a victorious life with inner confidence and freedom! Living in the power and realm of The Holy Spirit is not some mystical, obscure phenomenon but a living reality of confessing our Lord right from the moment we are born again, rejoicing in a life of victory! We discover the joy there is in serving Jesus!

The Challenge!

So then, where is the open confession of Jesus before all men from each born-again believer today? Do we confess Jesus by life and not by lip; at home but not at work; before God's people but not before the world? If we are to experience God's power and freedom from the shackles and weights of this world, we must never be ashamed to confess the Name of Jesus or to bear witness to His Saving grace before all men. We are not called to confess our church or denomination or our service for God; we are specifically chosen to confess The Lord Jesus Christ. The Holy Spirit is there to teach us and instruct us in the way we should go. As we, in faith and at God's command, speak His Word, God will work through us.

Moses had a challenge and became overwhelmed by fear and despair whilst leading the children of Israel out of Egypt. Upon reaching the banks of the Red Sea, he saw an impossible barrier before him, and furthermore, looking behind him, he could hear Pharaoh's chariots pounding towards them in pursuit, their dust rising to the sky. What was he to do? He cried out to God, then cried out again, but God was not going to do everything; He required something of Moses first!

Why is that? Why doesn't God just do the whole shebang whilst we watch Him? God very often requires our co-operation to speak words of faith for Him to act! That's the way it is! Not that we can do anything of ourselves, but God wants us to be part of the process of working together with Him! So, what happened next? The Lord said to Moses,

> *"Why do you cry to Me? Tell the children of Israel to go forward. But lift up your rod, and stretch out your hand over the sea and divide it."*
> **Exodus 14: 15-16**

We may not understand why God chooses to do things this way but know this – He does! As mentioned, God wants us to work by faith in Him and with Him! God requires us to have faith in Him, but more than that, He requires us to confess our faith with words, actions and deeds! It is a Divine order seen in the above Scripture from the Old Testament and is still required today!

The following Scripture shows us how important it is to confess God's Word by faith. It is one thing to hear and believe the Word of God but another, when the occasion calls, to confess it openly over our lives and speak it out publicly.

> *"But what does it say? **"The word is near you, in your mouth and in your heart"** (that is, the word of faith which we preach): that **if you confess with your mouth The Lord Jesus and believe in your heart that God has raised Him from the dead, you will be saved. For with the heart one believes unto righteousness, and with the mouth confession is made unto salvation."***
>
> **Romans 10: 8-10**

These Scriptures are clear! Here is the most foundational lesson in the importance and power of faith's confession found anywhere in the Bible! It is a principle to be carried forward from the very beginning of our life in Christ. Just as we appropriate God's Salvation through believing in our heart and confessing with our mouth, so He continues to work in our lives by the same means. That is, we continue to believe in our hearts and confess with our mouths! Let us begin and remain in this habit growing with active faith, believing in God's mighty power to support and help us. Let us speak and proclaim with our lips what our heart receives and believes from God's Word and all His promises. Remember,

*"...with the **heart one believes unto righteousness**, and with the **mouth confession is made unto salvation.**"*

Every person is called to live in the power and realm of God's Holy Spirit! That's the way it is! That's being born again! That's what it means to be born of The Spirit and not relying upon the flesh! Instead of living according to the flesh, we are to live according to The Spirit. We may know these things because of familiarity with the Scriptures, but the question is, *do we, in reality, also experience living in this realm?* So, in practice, we should not focus upon any adverse circumstances when they come along; instead, we should concentrate upon the Word of God that fits them! In this way, we are calling upon the realm of God's Spirit to help us!

Speak out with faith the chosen Words of God from the Bible that come to you and apply them to your mind's thinking! You will see what a transformation will take place! This is living according to The Spirit and not the flesh or our own human reasoning. Remember this principle only works by faith; faith, that is in God's Word, applying it to your circumstances!

Being in Position

In our daily lives, we are to stand in position before The Lord as vessels of honour and instruments of His righteousness.

We cannot suddenly be called upon by The Holy Spirit if we are not ready and in position. We need to acquire a lifestyle of waiting upon The Lord through reading His Word, meditating upon His Truths and prayerfully seeking His face. In this way, our focus is always upon The Lord and our prayer is one of expectation – *"Here I am Lord!"* Remember, the Word of God and our living knowledge and experience with Him is not just for our benefit but also for sharing with and ministering to others! That is, we give what we receive!

There was a servant of God called Ananias who lived in Damascus. He was in position, waiting upon God when The Lord spoke to him in a vision. He was told to go to the street called Straight and pray for a man called Saul of Tarsus to receive his sight. Even so, Ananias questioned The Lord regarding the mission, for he had heard how Saul had threatened and chained fellow servants of The Lord and had come to Damascus to do the same. However, despite this reservation, Ananias obeyed and did as God had commanded him, restoring Saul's sight through the power of prayer in the Name of Jesus.

The question is, am I in position before The Lord? Am I willing and ready to do His bidding? Do I believe that the prayer of faith will heal the sick according to God's will? Am I willing to relinquish my own thinking and reasoning if necessary and go as The Lord commands me?

If I, through my logic and reasoning, begin to analyse the mission of God, it will most likely never be accomplished! Therefore, being in position means I spend time in God's presence – as indeed Ananias did – to be sensitive to and conscious of The Spirit of God's voice. Remember, you can be God's vessel or instrument bearing His Word and prayer; God will do the rest!

Thus far, we have seen that to *"confess"* is a declaration and acknowledgement. We confess Jesus before men, and He promises us that He will confess us before His Father. We confess the Name of Jesus as Lord and acknowledge every facet of Him - for example; He is our Saviour, He is our healer, He is the King of Kings and Lord of Lords, He is our Redeemer, and so on.

There is a certain word in the Old Testament – *yadah* - and it appears a hundred or so times. It is often translated as *confess*, but it is translated as praise for the majority[4]. The words *praise* and *confess* are related.

To *praise God*, which is the main thrust of the word *yadah*, is to acknowledge who He is to you; what He means to you, what He has done for you: His Person, His Glory, His Holiness, and His Beauty! In so doing, you are attributing to God His very nature and bring glory and honour to His name! You are **confessing** Him and His attributes before men giving Him the recognition due as an act of thankfulness and worship! Hence, we shall see, there is liberating power in **true** praise and worship of God!

---

[4] Vine's Expository Dictionary

Interestingly, there are many occasions when we are acknowledging and confessing God for who He is of which we may not at first realise. For example, we use the secondary meaning of *yadah* when we *confess* our sins to God! This act of confession effectively acknowledges Him as the unique Person who alone can forgive sins, and therefore you are paying tribute to this aspect of Him. It was widely understood in the Old testament that confessing sin was a necessary prerequisite to being forgiven. This is well understood in the New Testament where it is written,

> *"If we **confess** our sins, He (Jesus) is faithful and just to **forgive** us our sins and to **cleanse** us from all unrighteousness."*
> **1 John 1:9**

Perhaps the next time you *praise The Lord*, whether privately or corporately, consider your *praise* as an act of acknowledging who Jesus is to you.

Thankyou Lord Jesus:

- *You are my Saviour,*
- *You have forgiven me all of my sin,*
- *You alone are the God of my salvation,*
- *You are faithful to me every day,*
- *You are Gracious and kind whenever I come to You,*
- *You are everything to me,*
- *You are all I need!*

Remember, giving verbal praise to The Lord is not, in itself, a magic formula. It all depends upon how we do it! For example, the Bible says we should pray, yes, but we can pray with our whole heart; we can pray more earnestly; we can pray in sincerity and truth – but we can also mouth words as from a book which can stem not from the inner person but from somewhere else! Remember, God knows our hearts and thoughts from afar off, so let us always come before Him in humility, sincerity, and truth. He knows what we need and is blessed when we truthfully pray for that! It will bring glory to His Holy Name and, most likely, bless those around you as The Spirit of God confirms the words you pray from a sincere contrite heart. Praise can most certainly have this effect; make no mistake! In fact, praise is a powerful means of bringing down the presence of God into a sphere inhabited by God and where He sets up His throne amongst His people! The following passage of Scripture is a perfect illustration and example of the above in a real-life occasion in the Old Testament and tells us what happened when the priests and Levites brought the Ark of the Covenant into Solomon's Temple:

> *"...it came to pass, when the trumpeters and singers were as one, to make one sound to be heard in praising and thanking The Lord, and when they lifted up their voice with the trumpets and cymbals and instruments of music, and praised The Lord, saying:"For He is good, For His mercy endures forever,"*

> *...that the house, the house of The Lord, was filled with a cloud, so that the priests could not continue ministering because of the cloud; for the glory of The Lord filled the house of God."*
> **2 Chronicles 5: 13-14**

If such things happened under the Old Covenant, should we not be able to experience our God inhabiting the praises of His born-again children, whose sins are forgiven and who have received the gift of eternal life? Ask yourself this question,

> *"Do I ever expect manifestations of God turning up in our praise times – or do I simply enjoy the melody and music?"*

God's people, Israel, would be familiar with the presence of the Shekinah glory of God whenever they lifted their voices as one and praised The Lord together! The following reference of *praise* in the well-known Messianic Psalm 22 refers to this phenomenon where God comes down in Glory upon His people.

> *"...But You are holy,* **Enthroned in the praises of Israel***..."*
> **Psalm 22:3**

If God is **enthroned in the praises of His people**, then this tells us that true worship is the key to entering His presence! The concept here is like the one mentioned above, where praise releases God's glory! Here is unquestionably one of the most exciting and remarkable things about honest and sincere praise! Praise will summon the presence of God, and therefore one can expect joy unspeakable and full of Glory!

"...in Your presence there is fullness of Joy!"
Psalm 16:11

Of course, it is true to say that God is present everywhere, but this is a specific manifestation of His Kingdom rule which enters the environment of praise.
In **Psalm 22:3**, the Hebrew word *yawshab* means *to inhabit* but is translated here as *enthroned*. It means:

To sit down; To remain; To settle. Take up residence in our lives.[5]

Here is the remedy for times when you feel alone, deserted, or depressed – Praise The Lord!

There are more examples in the Bible where Praise to God brought deliverance from the enemies of His people. Other examples in this book have shown us that God's people can live in the realm of The Holy Spirit, and we now see this also includes the act of praising The Lord!

[5] Strong's Concordance

Oh! That we could embrace these things without reservation or fear!

> *"Oh! that men would **praise The Lord** for his goodness, and for his wonderful works to the children of men! **Let them exalt him also in the congregation of the people,** and praise him in the assembly of the elders."*
>
> **Psalm 107:31-32 (KJV)**

Day 31

Our Position Seated with Christ in the Heavenly Places

> *"But God, who is rich in mercy, because of His great love with which He loved us, even when we were dead in trespasses, **made us alive** together with Christ (by grace you have been saved), and raised us up together, and **made us sit together in the Heavenly Places in Christ Jesus.**"*
> **Ephesians 2:4-6**

This Scripture is often used to describe our position in Christ as His born-again children, and today, the final day of our readings, I wish to explain what exactly this position is according to the Scriptures. It is another foundational truth that is often placed on the back burner of importance. It is rarely, if ever, preached even though its significance is profoundly breath-taking once understood.

One of the reasons this truth is uncommonly active in the minds of God's people could be that it is already understood that in the Name of Jesus, we access the most extraordinary power and authority in the universe! However, there is more! Our position in Christ will take us furthermore!

We are still thinking of our subject, *Living in the Power and Realm of The Holy Spirit,* and this is because everything is directly or indirectly related to The Spirit of God and His working in our lives. Let us firstly look at the following part in our opening Scripture.

> "...even when we were dead in trespasses, **made us alive** together with Christ..."

Notice that the words *'made us alive'* are also at the beginning of chapter 2 of Ephesians in verse 1.

> " And you, He **made alive**, who were dead in trespasses and sins."

Being made alive is where things begin because remember God had said to Adam and Eve-

> "...of the tree of the knowledge of good and evil you shall not eat, for in the day that you eat of **it you shall surely die."**
> **Genesis 2:17**

Consequently, we were once spiritually dead but have now been made spiritually **alive unto God** through faith in Jesus Christ! Being spiritually alive unto God through the new birth means we can learn and understand what was previously impossible to know before.

It is written,

> *"But the natural man does not receive the things of The Spirit of God, for they are foolishness to him; nor can he know them, because they are **spiritually discerned.**"*
>
> **1 Corinthians 2:14**

This truth should never be underestimated! Think about it; one moment, we are *spiritually dead,* and the next instant, we become *spiritually alive* upon receiving Jesus! This has implications everywhere in the Bible! For instance, we are translated from the Kingdom of Darkness into the Kingdom of Light, God's Kingdom! We are no longer citizens of this world but belong to God's Kingdom adopted into His family! We are His purchased possession, heirs of the promises and joint-heirs with Christ! This new spiritual relationship with God is worth meditating upon before we proceed any furthermore.

The final part of today's opening Scripture states,

> *"...and made us **sit together** in the Heavenly Places in Christ Jesus."*

So, initially, God made us spiritually alive, which was the first requirement then the Bible says we are,

> *"made to **sit together** in the Heavenly Places in Christ Jesus."*

What does this mean - *to sit together in the heavenly places...?*

Here is an important re-occurrence of the word *together*! The word *together* appears three times in this chapter which speaks of our union with Christ.

> *made us alive* **together** *with Christ* – ***verse 5***
> *and raised us up* **together** – ***verse 6a***
> *and made us sit* **together** – ***verse 6b***

In His **resurrection**
In His **ascension** and
In His **present rule** at God's right hand!

From this **place of partnership,** He grants that we **share** in the present works of His Kingdom's power!

This is termed our position in Christ!
"Heavenly Places"

(See: Ephesians:1: 3 and 20: Ephesians 3:10: Ephesians 6:12)

Heavenly Places does not refer to *Heaven* because it is our future home but rather refers to an *invisible realm* in the heavens that surrounds us. It is a sphere of spiritual activity.

> *"...what is the exceeding greatness of His power toward us who believe, according to the working of His mighty power which He worked in Christ when He raised Him from the dead and seated Him at His right hand in the* **heavenly places,** *far above all principality and power and might and dominion,* *and every name that is named, not only in this age but also in that which is to come."*

Ephesians 1: 19-21

The important thing to note here is that Christ is seated in the Heavenly Places *far above all principality and power and might and dominion.*
The New Testament also reveals this invisible hierarchy of evil powers who deceive and manipulate human behaviour. Whilst this activity is permitted because of man's free choice, Christ has overcome and triumphed over these powers, as it is written,

> *"...Having **disarmed principalities and powers**, He made a public spectacle of them, **triumphing over them**... "*
> **Colossians 2: 15**

The times are desperate in these last days because evil abounds[6], and the Bible says the love of many will wax cold because of it! Yet the Word declares what is happening and why.

> *"The Lord is not slack concerning His promise, as some count slackness, but is longsuffering toward us, **not willing that any should perish but that all should come to repentance.**"*
> **2 Peter 3:9**

---

[6] Living Victorious y in The Last days

On the one hand, evil is increasing, but God is in control. He desires as many as possible to come to a living knowledge of His Salvation. The child of God is commanded to be strong in The Lord and the Power of His might!

"Finally, my brethren, **be strong in The Lord** *and in the power of His might…"*
Ephesians 6:10

First, we need to realise that we are not told to be strong in our own strength. The word *power* refers to God's strength, not ours. We are called to be strong in His strength! God will **be our** strength, and as we believe this, we can boldly step out in faith, trusting in Him. Do you remember how God told Moses to step out or go forward on the banks of the Red Sea?!

God expects us to trust Him with a demonstrative, active faith! As we believe – so we receive! As we trust and go forward, letting go of any fear, embarrassment, or reservation, things will happen! God always expects us to do something even though it is God's power that ultimately does the work! We can so often get this wrong, thinking all we do is ask God, then sit back hoping He does something. Who taught us that concept? It is not how it works in the Bible! I must confront the battle head-on in prayer, calling upon God in Spirit and Truth speaking the Rhema [7]Word! I speak the words of authority in the Name of Jesus, and as The Spirit bears witness with my spirit, I can rest assured God will do it; God has got it! Then faith and prayer suddenly unite to become effective by the enabling power of The Spirit. This type of intercessory prayer is in alignment with the Word we have read today; that is, we are seated with Christ in the Heavenly Places both in union and partnership with Him! the Scripture means this when it says,

> "...*The effective, fervent prayer of a righteous man avails much."*
> **James 5:16b**

---

[7] Rhema- The spoken word; Logos – The written word

The second thing to realise is that,

> "... we do not wrestle against flesh and blood, but against principalities, against powers, against the rulers of the darkness of this age, against spiritual hosts of wickedness in the heavenly places..."
>
> **Ephesians 6: 12**

Read this passage carefully! We are not in conflict with any human person! We must realise this because the New Testament reveals the existence of an invisible hierarchy of evil powers who deceive and manipulate human behaviour! Therefore, being seated with Christ, we can pray against these powers of evil in the fullness of faith, believing and confessing the exact written Word of God!

So, we come to an end, and now we must believe and go forward with the enabling strength of God as He works within us and through us by His Word and His Spirit. A message from the Book of Hebrews speaks truthfully and pointedly.

> "...here have we no continuing city, but we seek one to come."
>
> **Hebrews 13:14** - KJV

The reality is there is one way forward for the child of God, and that is to live for Jesus as sojourners in this world fulfilling our Divine mission to preach the Word of His Salvation to all. But, at the same time, we are also told to be ready for His coming!

This book has sought to help us understand The Holy Spirit's work in our lives. From the moment we are born again, He is within us and desires our relationship to progress through our obedience to the Word of God, fulfilling His perfect, unique will for our life.

In all we seek to do, with The Spirit's guidance and help, there is a crucial matter never to lose sight of, namely, our Hope to come.

The coming of The Lord!

In closing, therefore, we will remind ourselves of this from the Scriptures.

*"Beloved, now we are children of God; and it has not yet been revealed what we shall be, but we know that when He is revealed, we shall be like Him, for we shall see Him as He is. **And everyone who has this hope in Him purifies himself, just as He is pure."***
1 John 3: 2-3

"And behold, I am coming quickly, and My reward is with Me, to give to every one according to his work."
Revelation 22:12,

"The grace of our Lord Jesus Christ be with you all. Amen"

Brian Reddish
March 2021

My Testimony

At the age of nineteen, I was living at home with my parents in a place called Langwith Junction in Derbyshire, England, which, as the name suggests, was a railway junction with sheds full of steam engines. It was a small village about one mile away from Shirebrook, a coal-mining market town.

By now, I was well into university studies at Chelsea College of Science, London, and I always looked forward to coming home during vacation times to see my then-girlfriend Pauline Marchant, who lived about seven miles away in Mansfield. She was awesome, and I considered myself very lucky! During one Easter vacation in the year 1966, I was ill in bed with the flu at my mum's house. I remember feeling quite low. My mother asked me to come to church with her as she said I would feel much better if I did. Being a dark, cold Wednesday evening, I reluctantly yielded to her pressure, feeling I had no option but to go; at least it was dark outside, and no one would particularly see me and where I was going! You see, I felt stupid and embarrassed going to a church.

Upon arrival at a medium-sized Pentecostal Church hall in Shirebrook, I saw no one there except two or three very elderly people - my mum never told me it was a Prayer Meeting! To my utter amazement, I recognised the man who stood at the front; it was Archie Roberts, and he owned a Fish and Chip shop in town!

I sat down sheepishly near the front, feeling very conspicuous and downcast. Soon Archie began to preach, having read out a verse or two from the Bible. He had read the passage from Matthew 16: 24-26, which says,

> "*Then Jesus said to His disciples, "If anyone desires to come after Me, let him deny himself, and take up his cross, and follow Me. For whoever desires to save his life will lose it, but whoever loses his life for My sake will find it. For what profit is it to a man if he gains the whole world and loses his own soul? Or what will a man give in exchange for his soul?"*"

He talked about a man being born into this world naked with nothing and leaving it in a similar fashion. I was always inspired by truth, and this I could not dispute – it was true! As he went on about life, the word began to speak to me - what would it profit me if I were to gain all the riches in the world only to die and then - that's it? I would leave everything behind! As a student, I had plans to live a full life, hopefully with a good job, but this word I was hearing shook me up to think more deeply and seriously - what was the meaning and purpose of my life? Where was I going? What was after?

Being prompted by mum's elbow, I stood up at the end of the meeting to walk out to the front and be prayed for to give my life to JESUS CHRIST.

I knew something spiritual took place that evening in the little hall; in fact, something supernatural! I had walked into the hall not knowing anything about God, but I walked out knowing this, GOD was VERY REAL; I knew because somehow, I had just met with HIM!! As I said, something spiritual happened - I don't know how - but it did!

From that day onward to this very day, fifty-two years later, God has been so real and personal to me. I had once said mockingly to my mum that if God is real, then He should talk with us and, for that matter, us with Him!

I instantly became hungry to read the Bible. I got to know Him more and more through His Word, which was opened up to me by His indwelling Holy Spirit! He gave me what I was looking for - a purpose and reason for life but, importantly, a real living relationship with God. So now I know this life is not the end but that it goes on with Him FOREVER!

BOOKS BY THE SAME AUTHOR

There Is a Balm in Gilead:
God's Healing Love, Grace and Compassion

A collection of 5 Inspiring Short Stories

The Dorothy McGuire Series

Dorothy McGuire: Book 1

Beautiful Dorothy McGuire carries a hidden, cruel, dark past – childhood sexual abuse!

Will she ever find release? Will be ever experience a normal relationship?

Dorothy McGuire: Book 2

An exciting continuation from Book 1 about how ordinary people's lives can be touched by an extraordinary God!

Dorothy McGuire:
Book 3 — The Final Chapter

This book brings to an end Dorothy's incredible journey and completes the MUST-READ trilogy!

Living Victoriously in the Last Days

A 31-day devotional

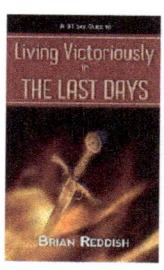

I Found Reality

An Autobiography

Living in His Presence

A 31-day devotional

All Books available in Print and e-book format.

Published by Caracal Books.

CONTACT THE AUTHOR

www.brianreddishbooks.uk

www.ingramcontent.com/pod-product-compliance
Lightning Source LLC
Chambersburg PA
CBHW041956080526
44588CB00021B/2757